No 1

MW01231099

5

— Secrets to a Free Life —

CHAD THOMPSON

This book is a gift of knowledge for anyone looking for the right path to both monetary and spiritual growth

In keeping with this book's message, a portion of the author's profits from this book will be donated to a non-profit, charitable cause.

Booking Information:
To Book Chad Thompson for your next speaking engagement, please contact:

workwithchad@yahoo.com
www.chadethompson.com
www.mlmclasses.com
All social media: @nomore925

1st ed.
ISBN 978-0-692-67306-5

DEDICATION

First, I *would like to dedicate this book to all my believers, all my friends offline and online, all of my old and present mentors, and everyone who has given me words of encouragement over the years. This is for all of you because if it weren't for you all, I would still be writing this book. Thanks to all the people across the world who have been following my NoMore925 campaign and getting inspired. This is for you.*

Secondly, this book is for my newborn son, Emir Estes Thompson. I want to show my one-year-old son that anything and everything is possible if you design your own life. You can do anything you put your mind to, son, and daddy will forever love you. He has motivated me to go to the next level in my life.

Thirdly, I dedicate this book to my mother, Denise LaFranque, who helped me put this book together and spent countless hours reading and editing every word, and encouraged me to go deeper and to give all of you 'the real'. You have always been my #1 Fan and showed true love and tough love, all at the same time. I can never repay you for all you have done for me. The least I can do is make the rest of your life the best of your life.

Last but not least, thank you to all the people who said I wouldn't make it in life. I believe you all are known as haters. Thank you so much. It's because of you guys that this is still just the beginning of history, and there's plenty more coming in the future. Thanks for keeping me on my job.

ACKNOWLEDGMENTS

God
My Grandma
My Grandpa
My Mother
My Father
My sisters and brothers
My Uncle
All my cousins
Coach Bush
Charlie Morgan
Ant
Ray
Malik
Corey B
Gerald Bass
Catrina Williams
Soraya Barker
Shatorri Phillips
Mr. Wayne
Bree Kemp

TABLE OF CONTENTS

FOREWORD

I have never met a more tenacious, courageous, and fearless visionary other than Chad Thompson. Most people make big plans and never obtain them but Chad blasts through obstacles that would stop corporate executives and seasoned professionals. His grit, will power, and consistency are legendary. His success is not by way of any easy path or crumb snatching.

Chad is resourceful and creative. He is not afraid to lean on his friends or collaborate with his enemies. He is one part Machiavelli, one part Malcolm, and one part Reginald Lewis. He is loved by his friends because he is loyal beyond words. He is admired by his haters because of his resiliency and his championship disposition. He is a machine—each day challenging himself to get better and become Chad 2.0 and beyond. He is a soldier, entrepreneur, and a visionary. He is always willing to pay the price for success and help others along the way.

He is unstoppable.

He is the storm.

He is a champion.

— Thomas W. Felder II, Esq.

CHAPTER 1

Rich People Weren't Always Rich

When I was twelve years old, I never stopped dreaming of being rich. Today, at 27 years old, I know that your dreams shouldn't match your income, but back then I was only dreaming and didn't care about my income. This is the story of how I went from a boy to a man, a bum to a boss, a chump to champ, and an employee to a C.E.O. I was able to turn $29 into $800k, all from a cell phone and a laptop. That process was how I developed the name that became the beginning of my blessings: *NoMore925*.

Despite the success that I have been blessed with, my journey to prosperity was rough to say the least. I was born in Philly and raised in Atlanta. Ever since I can remember, it has always been just me and my mom, 'the dynamic duo'. My mother, a hard worker, had always made great money at her jobs – close to six figures – until one day, out of nowhere, she got sick. Money was always tight from then on. But no matter how many jobs my mom had, I remained positive. When I was growing up, she always made sure I had the first if not the best of everything, but when she got sick, she had to lie in bed, unable to work for nearly a year. We were suddenly in the direst of circumstances. Now, I don't want you to feel sorry for me, but I do want you to know my real story so you can understand my grind and where I come from. One of the most important lessons I learned on my journey is that stories have power. I want you to understand why the *NoMore925 Mentality* is important, so bear with me. I know that, in my story, you'll find something that relates to your own life, and you'll be inspired.

I wasn't the type to beg people for things. I was always a deep thinker—even today, people who know me personally know that my mind wanders in mid conversation—so as a latch-key kid, I noticed a lot of things about myself and the world at a young age. I saw that keeping all your eggs in one basket impacts your life and the lives of your children. I started thinking, *how could she work all her life and have her entire world destroyed with one illness?* I thought, *if she had one main source of income with a few freelance jobs, and losing that main source put us back this many levels, where would we be if she hadn't had the extra jobs?* We couldn't predict when my Mom was going to be sick, or when something tragic might happen to us. I noticed this before most kids do, and it haunted me.

We had been celebrating in our brand new house for about a month when mom said she had to go into the hospital for a quick procedure and would be home in a couple of days. She went in for her surgery on September 9, 2001 but didn't wake up until September 13, 2001. She missed the 9/11 terrorist attacks. When I went to visit her, I knew with one look that whatever was going on, it was serious, but no one was telling me anything. In just those few short days, she had close to 10 surgeries. She had tubes everywhere—tubes with blood, medicine, food, and even one hooked up to a machine to help her breathe. I spent a couple of nights in the hospital with her, but after a while, she didn't want me staying there. She understood that environment mattered and that this wasn't healthy for me.

Almost a year later, my mother was still in the hospital, nowhere near getting better. I had supportive aunts and cousins in the area, but I was living with my coach because he lived closest to my high school. I was homeless with a brand new house—the irony.

One day, I went to visit and she wasn't in her room. Just as panic started to sink in and I was on my way to the nurse's station to find out where she was, I saw her walking down the hall with someone.

I was so happy to see her up. As she got closer, I started to laugh so hard I almost cried.

I could tell my mom was getting better when I went to visit her for Thanksgiving and she was actually plotting an escape and asked for my help. I knew boredom was really taking a toll when I walked into her room and she was just staring out of the window. When I asked what was wrong, she replied she was counting how many cars were going through the drive-thru at the Steak-N-Shake across the street. She actually escaped a total of three times that I can remember.

One particular day sticks in my memory, and I want you to use it to catch the essence of the *NoMore925 Mentality*. Once, I walked into the hallway to visit my mom, and I heard a woman crying loud, "I wish I had got in here earlier!" I found out later that she had just lost her dad, and because of her work schedule, she couldn't afford to take time off before his big surgery. He died on day three. The family came the first day, but because of her *job*, she missed her father's last days. She blamed herself, her job and her husband. He was the one that told her to take off those days, but she believed they needed both sources of income to pay the bills. She truly believed that her dad would make it until the surgery. Her *job mentality* convinced her that work was more important, and that she couldn't afford to do otherwise.

Mom and I were trapped in the same situation. We were forced to sell our brand new house that we had owned for 3 ½ years but only lived in for less than a year, and move into a two-bedroom duplex. We lived off food stamps and, to some degree, the generosity of those around us. I remember my girlfriend at the time worked at KFC. For months she had the responsibility of closing the store down and brought us the 'end of the day' chicken and sweet tea. We were struggling...badly. I even remember sleeping on a futon with jackets on because the duplex had no central heat and the space heaters didn't produce much heat, either.

These experiences taught me early on that I didn't want to work some job for the rest of my life. I was great at football, but no matter how great football was, I knew if the pro life didn't happen for me, then the job life would. But in my mind, my mom's illness had me thinking "What if?" early on. *What if football didn't work out? What if I get sick and my money stops, how can I help my mom out?* I decided to take some construction courses as a Plan B. Even at 14 years old, I knew if I could use the gifts God gave me, which were my hands, I would be successful.

Mom worked hard to give me every advantage she could, even with limited resources. As my school years went on, she was slowly getting on her feet by doing substitute teaching while studying for her license. With the help of coaches who recognized my talents, and school administrators, she got a teaching job and I was able to attend a prestigious school. She was determined to help me succeed in every way she knew how. Until I got my license and my own car, my mother drove me all the way across town every day, sometimes four to six times a day to my new school. Sometimes when she had freelance jobs, she arranged to drop me off at the home of one of my football buddies at 4am so I could catch the bus from there.

In those years of driving back and forth, I noticed I was living a double life and saw how different life could be. When I started driving all the way home from my rich school on the east side to our small duplex in the hood, I saw both sides of the world in which I was living: my high school friends versus my hood friends, and prosperity versus poverty. Mom always told me in order to grow in life, different parts of your past must die. I didn't know at the time how important that lesson would be but that's also where my balance came from and where I learned to communicate with all kinds of people.

My home environment was totally different culturally than my school environment had been. I was the only one in my neighborhood without a felony. I was introduced to machine guns early and the people on the block had them at a young age. I was the only one out of all the kids with a curfew, and the only conversations that occurred were about childish activities and how the government didn't care about us. That's when I realized that environment is better than will power! Many of my hood friends were smart, but their surroundings had made their beliefs small. Work ethic isn't nearly enough to succeed; you have to believe in yourself.

My mother wasn't the only major influence at that time. My construction teacher, Mr. Fisher, was a strict man who played no games in his classroom. I was popular, well-liked, and the class clown, but bending pipe, cutting wood, and using power tools came naturally. I hated reading and struggled in all the other subjects in school, but building and using my mind to figure things out were right up my alley. I once asked Mr. Fisher for a dollar to hit up the vending machine. In all honesty, I was only 25 cents short. He told me he never lent people money because wealthy people don't do that, and he gave me a book called *The 48 Laws of Power* instead. I laughed because he and I both knew I didn't like to read. He told me if I just went through chapter by chapter it would change my life. He was right. Before looking at the title of the book, I opened it and landed on *Law 10*. It said: "Infection: Avoid the unhappy and the unlucky." It basically said that other people's misery drains you, and that the unfortunate draw misfortune upon themselves. We as a people have to break the cycle and start our families off with a better advantage, because if we don't, it will be harder for them to avoid mimicking what they see us doing. Coming from the bottom, I experienced first hand that kids believe that if you aren't exceptionally talented, your chances of breaking the cycle are slim to none.

Immediately, that message hit me like a ton of bricks. Every time I left high school to go back to the hood, I heard all these sad stories, but when I was in high school, on the good side of town, I heard the possibilities of the future. I started noticing that the majority of the folks at home thought successful people only got there by luck, and that mindset drained me of positive thinking. My teacher told me if I finished that book before our final test, he would take me to a construction expo. I said, "You have a challenge!"

Overtime, Mr. Fisher's tone became more serious, "At your age Chad, if you really live your life of these principles, because you're already mature, you can do and be great in this world."

I told him that I had decided I wasn't going to college to play football. I had a shot to play for Southern Mississippi State but wouldn't see the field until my junior year. My coach wanted me to go to college and play, but I felt in my heart that I couldn't wait that long. I had to help my sick mom more than ever because her health was getting worse and the job she had to settle for was way too stressful. I decided to go full-time into construction. *Law 25* helped me with my choice: "Recreate yourself: Do not accept the roles that society foists on you, forge a new identity, command attention!"

As the months of my senior year passed by, passion for football started going away and my passion for earning money increased. When I started high school, a football career was all I considered because everyone kept me hyped up about my talents. Even though my vision was clearer than everyone around me, thoughts of 'what if' started happening again, so I focused on my construction and my buying and selling skills. I had speakers, CD players, rims, anything you needed to be cool, and I sold them everywhere. I also finished second in my construction class and landed my own seat at the career construction expo.

Out of all the teachers I've had, Mr. Fisher was the only one to inspire me to push myself. It meant a lot to me when he said, "The way you are planning for your future in construction is amazing." I told him thanks for dealing with me and my attitude in the beginning, and for not giving up on me. I always refer to my notes from the book he gave me to keep me grounded. Just seeing the expression on his face when I finished reading it brought such joy to my heart because I overcame the challenge by utilizing *Law 23*: "Concentrate your forces. Look for sources to elevate you."

After school I had a job waiting for me because I tested so high at the expo. That experience was my first encounter with a real millionaire. The owner of Whitehead Electric said to me personally that, once I turned 18, I would have a job as an electrician. Knowing that helped me get through some tough times, because I wouldn't turn 18 for another five months. I told the millionaire that he hadn't seen anything yet—wait until I take *this* seriously. He laughed and said he loved my confidence. In my mind, I was thinking about *Law 30*: "Make your accomplishments seem effortless!" Your actions must seem natural and executed with ease. Teach no one your tricks, or they will be used against you. You have to recognize when you meet someone out of your tax bracket and make an impression.

See, if you don't know that the *job mentality* and the *NoMore925 Mentality* exist, you will go through the same situation over and over, working for multiple people, thinking you need multiple streams. What you're really doing is working backwards. Don't get me wrong—it's okay to have a job. What I've learned is that it's not okay to *only* have a job. The lack of belief in yourself limits you.

This story that you're reading is real, and I have to tell you, I have never gone this deep into my story before. The purpose of this book is to challenge your way of thinking and show you how to overcome life's twists and turns. I'm sure you've been sick before and it has affected your income. Think about this, when that happened, did you have the *job mentality* or the *NoMore925 Mentality*? I want to help you discover what type of person you are. If you want to shift away from waiting on the age to retire, remember that it takes income to retire.

I have put this masterpiece of a book together just for you! On these next few pages, I dropped all the nuggets you need, pre-dipped in sauce, so enjoy this book and use it to assist you along your journey. I welcome you into my life, and I forewarn you that it's about to get real so don't miss the messages!

CHAPTER 2

The Real World and My Introduction to the Job Mentality

I finally turned 18 and was ready to work. I worked construction for three years, thinking I was making good money, a mere $10-$13/hour, and learning as much as I could about the job from my bosses. But what I really wanted was to *be* the boss. Yes, I was making money, but I had to ask myself a serious question that I believe no one ever really asks themselves: do I want to *make* money or *have* money? Making money takes forever and is very time consuming. Most people go 10, 20, or 40 years only making money, and by the time they realize they need it, it's too late and they're burnt out. Everybody makes it, but only a small percentage *have* it.

I went to work every day with another purpose: figure out how I can flip my money situation and start *having* it. When I looked at the bigger picture, I realized the only people who had money in their bank accounts were the people next door to the owner's office. I wanted to be like Pete Foster so bad—an owner, and a man who put his kids in the position to have a great life. Then I looked at myself and realized, *I have no money, I barely graduated high school. All my friends are broke and only want to party. How in the world could I be him?* I told my hood friends I wanted to be like the owner at my job, and they missed the whole point. The first thing they said was "Why you wanna be like a White man?" I quickly shut all that down because I learned early if you argue with fools from the outside looking in, you are both fools in the end. I let them make jokes, but it was at that time that I began to let people from outside of my normal culture into my life.

The first thing I had to do was figure out how to get in my boss's mind. Humility, in my opinion, is recognizing something you don't have and asking questions until you have it. Some people never learn how to change their finances because they are too busy prejudging the opportunity that they really should be learning more about, or judging the people they should be learning from. *Law 3* taught me to "Conceal your Intentions: Keep people off balance by never revealing your purpose behind your actions, if they have no clue they can't defend." In order to get into my boss's head, I needed to be around him more. The only way I could get around him was to volunteer to come in early in the morning to pick up the trash cans and clean off the Project Manager's desk. But the crazy thing is, he never came into the office early but somehow made the most money! I was always the second or third person there and had the least amount of money.

But one day, a chance encounter sent me on the path that would change everything. When I went home, I stopped by the gas station and saw a girl I used to work with, Shatorri. During our conversation, she made a comment about a job being like modern day slavery, and it stuck with me. I paused for a moment because the day I had at work felt somewhat like that. Before I left, Shatorri invited me to her house the next day. I thought this was my lucky day because I needed new friends with new mindsets. I told her I had to work, but asked if I could still come if I was a little late—she said yes. Not even worried why she wanted me at her house, I said I'd see her tomorrow.

The next morning, I showed up to work and what do you know, the owner was there. I asked him to give me one tip for how to be like him and he said, "You only get two opportunities in life to be wealthy, and Chad, you don't know if you already missed both of them. Take plenty of risks in your lifetime or you will live to regret it." That was all I could think about all day. After clock-watching for eight hours, it was finally time for me to get off and meet Shatorri.

CHAPTER 3

The Text That Changed Everything

Shatorri hit me up the next day and said "Don't forget to come and dress business casual." I looked at the phone and said to myself, *All I have is that one suit from the eighth grade. I don't have business clothes, but I can't let her know that. I'm going anyway.* She texted me the address and I thought, boy this is far away. I started thinking about gas and how my car was a hooptie and that it probably wouldn't make it. All kinds of excuses ran through my head. But I wasn't going to get out of it so easily.

At that moment my friend Ray called and said, "What are you doing? Let's grab some drinks, I'm in your area." That was all the push I needed. I quickly told him to come pick me up instead and that I had some girls that want us to come over. *Law 13*: "When asking for help, appeal to people's self interest, never to their mercy or gratitude!" Conceal within your request something that will benefit him. It wasn't lying, technically. I knew that Ray would definitely be interested if women were involved and bringing him along trumped all the excuses I'd been making for myself.

When we arrived, there were only eight other people there, and they were all older men in their fifties. Fortunately, Ray wasn't mad because Shatorri said he was cute and that we were about to learn how to make some money. Shatorri flashed us her phone, and it was a check for $3,000. My eyes lit up at the idea of making that much money. That was more than I made at my full-time job! She was in the same situation, but she made the decision that this was her last week working for someone else. Then her manager walked in and said we were about to start. I didn't care what he was about to sell me; if it could pay me more than what my job was paying, I was down to try it. I remembered what the owner at my job had just told me earlier that day, "take plenty of risks so you don't miss your two chances to be wealthy."

I was all ears. The next thing I knew; I was being introduced to Network Marketing. I'd never ever heard of it, but the speaker said I could be my own boss, retire within 2-5 years, get rich, work from home without an alarm clock, and help so many others live a balanced life.

I felt honored to have this information at a young age. I'd heard a lot of people say, "If only I knew then what I know now," and here it was, my head start. I was all in! All I could see was my mom's face, that stupid futon, and that $3,000 check. I remembered something my pastor had said a couple of Sundays ago that didn't make sense then but did now: "Anything you fail to recognize will exit your life." I though to myself, *I don't understand it all, but I can't be skeptical and broke, so I'm going to try it. I could always stay an electrician if it didn't work*. Shatorri was younger than me—only 19 years old—and I came to find out, the huge house that we were all meeting at was hers! That was all I needed to know.

When Charles, Shatorri's manager, asked who in the room was interested in getting started, no hands went up but mine. "Could I start tonight?" I shouted. I couldn't wait to join! Next, I had a conversation with the speaker for a while about my goals.

Charles asked me, "What is the biggest room in the world?"

Being funny, I said, "This living room."

He laughed for two seconds and said, "The biggest room in the world is room for improvement."

There comes a point in life when we have to choose which voice we listen to. He told me that I shouldn't listen to just anyone, because they will try to steal my dream. I assured him that I am a leader. I would get in this business regardless of who likes it or not.

He told me that was great that I had that amount of ambition because "I cannot change your life until I change the voice you trust."

That day, I gained a mentor and learned what mentorship really means. There's a big difference between a boss and a mentor. Because you and your boss work together, he won't honor your personal goals. A boss can only see the assignment he gives you. A mentor knows your weaknesses and is willing to endure them to unleash your strengths and your gifts. Have more mentors than bosses and watch how life unfolds for you. How you see yourself determines your conduct and self-worth. Your similarities create your comfort, and your differences decide your importance in the economy. Your new goal, once you join, must be bigger than you.

But as soon as I was ready to jump in, I hit a snag. It cost $500 to get my business started, and with empty pockets and pennies in my bank account, I was hurt, but more determined than ever.

CHAPTER

The Negative Seeds That Follow

W hen we left the meeting, I was so fired up! Ray thought it was a well-put-together scam, "How you going to get people to give you $500? No one has that kind of money to give up like that."

I saw that as an obstacle, not a problem. "Why do 70% of employees have less than $1,000 in their bank accounts?" I said. He simply said it was because they don't manage their money. I told him no, it's because taxes and the system are set up with an imbalance between the *cost of living* and the *determined worth* by employers, and no one can get ahead.

Then he brought it all back home again with, "Okay Chad, well how are you going to get people to spend $500 in a down economy?" I didn't have the answer to that yet, but I knew I would discover the *how* later—right now I knew my *why*! I was just so happy I showed up and couldn't wait to tell my mom that when God wants to bless you, He brings the right people into your life. I believe I ran into my old friend Shatorri for a reason.

Charles told me I would run into dream stealers, but I hadn't expected it to happen this fast. As soon as I left the meeting my own friend wanted my dream shot down! In my mind I was thinking, *how do I have friends to club with, but no friends to do business with*? As far as your friends are concerned, first they'll ignore you, then they'll ridicule you, then they'll fight you, and then you'll win. You can't force chemistry to exist where it doesn't in the same way you can't deny it when it does.

When I got home it was late, and I was already in trouble. Mom had asked me to buy her a Milky Way and some Reese's Cups while I was out, and I'd forgotten them in all the excitement. I remembered as soon as I walked in the house, but it was too late, and of course she was right there on the couch asking, "You got my candy right?" We were already off to a bad start.

I said, "I have something better than candy, Mom."

I told her all about my new opportunity, but she wouldn't have it. We argued, and I went to my room pissed that my mother, who has always supported me, was acting like this. This was something new. My "What if?" thoughts started again. *What if I don't make any money? What if this is a scam? What if no one joins?* So I called my girlfriend at the time and asked her to loan me the money.

To my surprise, on my way to work the next morning, my girlfriend called and said she didn't believe in it, but for me she'd let me use her credit card. I called Shatorri immediately, and on December 12, 2010, I joined Network Marketing at 21 years old with $29 in my bank account and pennies in my pocket.

This was great, but I still had some more negatives to overcome. When I got to work the next morning, as I was cleaning my boss's trash can out, he walked in and said, "What's up Chad? Tell me something new."

I looked up with a smile and said, "Sir, I am now a business owner and can help you save money on your gas bill, and all your phone lines." He asked for more information, and I gave it to him, but at the end of the day he turned me down. He told me only the people at the top of those kind of pyramid businesses make money, but he gave me something else—it was his old leather briefcase. He said it would hold my laptop and paper work. He made his first million with that briefcase. Even though I took it, I was sad to realize that he was at the top of his company and I was still at the bottom. My common sense kicked in and I told myself, wait—I'm at the top now!

I started doing research on pyramid schemes. Because those words popped up often as I talked about my new business, I learned that all business structures are formed with levels. Even my job had levels, and I was at the bottom. I worked harder than my bosses, and they got paid more, so why doesn't anyone call this electrical business a pyramid scheme? My hunger for that top level only increased. I no longer wanted to work way harder than a boss who made way more.

I couldn't rest that night. I had discovered this huge truth and decided not to act like it was ok. That's when I discovered the word *leverage*, meaning that I have the ability to influence other people's actions. My co-workers laughed at me and thought I was getting played left and right, but I knew I wasn't settling and wanted more for my life and the lives of others. I had a good laugh picturing myself on an island while they were still working in the warehouse. In the meantime, I just joined in their laughter because, 'He who laughs last, laughs best'.

CHAPTER

The Process

As I started on my search for more leverage in my life, I realized something: most people think that making a lot of money is hard, but it's actually much harder to stay broke. Have you ever been in traffic, so frustrated that you thought you would never get to your destination? As you're reading this guide, I hope you realize that you're no longer in traffic. The period of being held back, beat-up, blocked, or stuck, will only last for a moment. Every traffic jam in your life will end if you keep the faith and believe in yourself. Never confuse your timing for God's.

More than *feeling* how I wanted, *living* how I wanted was still most important. I often needed time by myself to reflect and focus; that perspective was key for me. I looked at the briefcase that my rich boss gave me, and as I sat there, I put my head in my hands and cried. I was a grown man living in America and couldn't properly help my own mom. You see, it wasn't the weekly notices from bill collectors letting me know that our bills were overdue, nor was it the daily calls I received from the collectors. My fuel came from the emotional impact of my mom's embarrassment that she couldn't pay her bills and her feeling that she'd failed in life. You have to be about your business, and you have to remember why you're so passionate. I call this the *"mad decision."* My mom used to tell me I was her only accomplishment, but as much as I told my mom that I'm all she needs, I couldn't really help her. I had breath in my body to make a change, but I delayed the process and kept hoping for things to get better. That fear of letting my family down struck a fire in me that I will never forget.

Reflection helped me come to an important realization and I analyzed what I was up against: negative friends, a skeptical mom, a doubtful girlfriend, and my boss's view that I was in a pyramid scheme. I started thinking about Ray and *Law 43*: "Work on the hearts and minds of others: Seduce others into wanting to move in your direction. Soften up resistance by working on their emotions and what they fear." Then the light bulb clicked! I would play on people's emotions, what they fear, and attract them into the business. People are afraid of making the wrong decision. Many do not even realize that they are on a path in which only 1% have money. If I can show them the truth about the route they are already taking, they will at least have a chance to make a decision to improve their lives.

The next challenge was my mom. *Law 38*: "Think as you like but behave like others. Share your originality and uniqueness only with people who appreciate you," was the best example for this situation. Everyday when I came home, I didn't mention the business; I would only let her hear me working. My goals were to make some money first, then take her out to eat and whip out my MLM company card. This was an important goal for me because I'd always thought that most parents are hypocrites. I always find it funny how parents send their kids to school to get a good education, then put pressure on them to get good grades, force them every day to do their homework, and then when the school rewards the kids with honor roll, they go and put it on their cars and start bragging about how smart their kids are. I never understood why the parents lost their own juice. When did they stop bragging about themselves? They should do the same things they expect of their kids. When the report card of their adult lives come home and they don't make the honor roll, who punishes them?

Students have to show their grades to see if they really passed the test. What if parents had to pass the 'life test', and were forced to have a life coach? Ask yourself: have you really lived life to the fullest, or did you settle for a C-average lifestyle? Parents, it's time to make A's in the real world—an above-average lifestyle. Let's never settle for the C-average lifestyle just like we wouldn't let our kids settle. I was in the middle of a process, and I only wanted my mom to see the end result. I determined that there are five smaller steps within this step to accomplish:

1. Change Your Mindset

Success is possible when you attach yourself to the right vehicle, but every great professional was just a beginner at one time, and every great product or company began as just an idea. It's not about how far along you are, but how hard you are willing to work to finish what you started.

Charles, my new mentor, called to welcome me to the team and said we needed to meet as soon as possible. I had a lot of questions about the direction I would go with my business. I remember telling him about some of the negative people I ran into as soon as I left the meeting. He said, "Wow, and you still joined? You might just be strong enough to survive this challenge."

In the hood, just to survive is to overcome. So when I asked him, "How hard will this journey be?" and he replied, "However hard you make it. It's

90% mental and 10% physical," I knew that this too I would overcome. If you reach out to your mentor every day, your mindset will be forced to change.

To lead an army, you have to be battle tested, and the army at MLM (Multi-Level Marketing) is full of volunteers. That last nugget from my mentor stood out so much, I followed up with, "If this is 90% mental, it seems that everybody would volunteer to participate in their own rescue, right?"

He replied, "You know what Harriet Tubman said, don't you?" He told me that she would have freed more slaves, if only they knew they were slaves, "The key, Chad, is to discover your 'WHY' and never attach your goals to a person who joins your team defiantly." People make it hard, being emotional about minor things, and never getting serious about what is major. Which is where consistent action comes into play: making new friends everyday. It's crazy that some people feel that 2-5 years in business is a long time to get rich, but don't feel that 40 years at a job is a long time to stay broke.

Charles also told me I could no longer 'major in minor' or *spend major time with minor people*. It means that I shouldn't let every disappointment, big or small, make a difference in my life or let everything make me mad or emotional. He said I had to recruit myself first before I could try to sign anyone else up.

Still baffled I said, "Excuse me Sir but I paid my money—I did recruit myself!"

He laughed and told me that when you recruit yourself, you do what is required, not your best. If you don't do this, the giving part will be too far fetched and out of reach. Everyone wants to give more and help others, but they don't save themselves first.

So how do you save yourself? First, you have to be 100% coachable—do what you are told as soon as you are told and don't get stuck in your old habits. The amount of time it takes to get the message into your brain and manifest into reality makes a huge difference. The only reason you're not living the life of your dreams is because of the nonsense stories you tell yourself. Not being coachable from the beginning can delay growth in your opportunity. You must deal with your inner truths, even if most are bad.

To do this, I had to learn to look at information from the perspective of "What haven't I done yet?" instead of "What do I do?". When you figure out what you haven't done, do it that same day. Looking at my journey for instance, I'm finding out that *staying* successful is harder than getting to *be* successful.

Be willing to fail and be tested outside your comfort zone. This is huge because in traditional businesses, it takes a while to profit. As a matter of fact, I believe that 80% of most new businesses fail in the first 2-3 years. Donald Trump said his failures led to his success. Warren Buffet also noted that he failed a couple of times before becoming successful. These two powerful men proved that you can always bounce back from failure.

The stress of possible failure will make you or break you. Mastering stress requires the ability to distance yourself from the present moment and think about the past and the future. As far as the future is concerned, the further you can see, and the more steps ahead you can plan, the better your day will go...trust me.

Here's a success tip for dealing with stress: when the past comes calling, hit the ignore button. As long as it has nothing new or positive to say, don't listen to the past. I propose that you try a seven-day challenge. As the coachable reader that you are, you should try this challenge because as you go hard for your dreams, you have to be confident enough that God is working on you and for you. I promise you that your dreams will cost you more than you and your spouse have in your bank accounts. That is why the *7 Day Nothing Negative Challenge* is key. It's a, "I won't say, think, or do anything negative for 7 days straight" challenge. It's a complete all around test of will that everyone should do.

2. Earn And Learn At The Same Time

I was beginning to understand this new journey a little more. I knew that I first had to work on me because I was in a whole new element. Now, some of us can't even believe that we were designed to live big. Most people, including myself at that time, feel we are lucky to have what we have ($15-$25/hr) if we keep comparing ourselves to other people. Personally, I was ready to raise my personal bar and focus on a better life.

The grind would be completely different from anything I'd ever done. I knew I had to improve my people skills because this 'Opportunity to Be Free' was serious, and I wasn't playing around. I had to build a list of people without judgment, because when you prejudge, you already say no for the people, which is something a lot of rookies do. In the beginning, the first focus on your list should be *quantity* over *quality*. You see, practice makes permanent, and having more people will give you more experience and opportunities for improvement.

It took me about three weeks to do my list. When I checked in with Shatorri she said, "Chad, I really though we would be further along than this by now."

I said "I have my list ready, I just need to review the scripts and learn the rebuttals."

She responded by saying, "Success loves speed, and it doesn't matter if you know all the answers to everything. What matters is how much experience you gain while in the process. They just paid me again and I though about you." It seemed that Shattori knew exactly how to push my buttons and at the same time, teach me a lesson in leadership. I learned the importance of motivating my partners by using the right words *and* actions. I got right on it—making calls and taking massive action fast before the negative self-talk could kick in again.

I started moving forward, but there were constant challenges. My first ten calls were horrible. I had the script right in front of me but got nervous and didn't stick to it. Shatorri told me, "It's great that you are at least trying. Your failures will put you and keep you ahead of the people who never try. One day your failures will help you stand out so much you will become needed to the masses." I also heard that my auntie had called family members and told them not to answer my calls. This didn't make me mad, it just made me more determined to make it. I quickly remembered *Law19*: "Know who you're dealing with; don't offend the wrong person. Choose your victims and opponents carefully, never offend or deceive the wrong person. Look out for wolves in lamb's clothing."

A lot of the skills I learned in the streets were transferrable to business. My friends, family, and co-workers all said it sounded great but still did nothing to support me. I made zero dollars my first month and doubt hit me when my girl asked me if I had her money yet. But still holding on to faith, I told her it was coming. This was an amazing moment in my life—the pressure was really on. Back in my football days, I always heard that pressure makes some people break and some people break records. Pressure kills procrastination.

Soon after, I started to feel the shift happening, going from employee to owner, but no one joined me my first month. My family said I needed to get a second job or try to go back to college. I even invited a couple people out to see a presentation and no one even showed up. I got so disappointed that I wasn't operating in my 'faith zone'. I realized I couldn't believe everything everyone told me, only what they showed me. Don't talk to prospects for value or validation. You just have to keep going like RoboCop—half human and half machine—no emotion, just a script. I had to figure out how to *reduce the changes of inconvenience*. I was so determined to show them, and besides, the support I was getting from my up-line at the time was what really mattered. It helped me stay away from victim thinking and stay the course of my *NoMore925 Mentality*.

3. Understand The Business

The only thing that matters is your level of understanding. Understanding that failure is needed to succeed is hard because in school if you fail, you get held back, in football if you fail, you're benched, and at work if you fail, you're fired. So I was, of course, scared to fail! That's why the shift I felt in my mindset was so important to maintain. To achieve the *NoMore925 Mentality*, I had to get comfortable with failing.

I also had to learn the *slowing down to speed up* process. In business, you're not going to win 24/7. If business never slowed down, then you would never take the time to check every area of your life for growth. My natural tenacity, a.k.a. beast mode, had its moment when my energy level was low. This is when I needed and received many talks from my up-line and mentor to help me get through a few roadblocks.

Staying plugged in and communicating is the only reason I didn't quit. It helped to keep my mindset strong. Communication skills are key to networking, but you have to be mindful of who you're communicating with. I learned how to learn from strangers, and it took my 'faith zone' to be around different types of people. At the same time, I had to stop hanging out with people for the hell of it. This is huge if you're a person who is easily bored and don't like being alone. I was also one of those people who didn't trust others easily, which made it even harder to reach out to strangers to grow my new circle.

Before I built my network, I had no influence; but gaining power requires looking at the world a certain way. Dreams and goals are the only difference between people who do nothing and those who do something. Don't get caught up in how you do things. That's a trap most people fall into. Most of my MLM students feel like their lives are 'laid', meaning all together and unchangeable. Knowing there's another level you can get to in life should be your call to action, your driving force, your 'why'. You should always feel that you deserve a better life.

4. Always Network And Market

Shifting from employee to owner is hard. Most people want to have a successful life, but all they actually do is sit around and watch Netflix like they have already made it. It's time to get up and hustle like your job is about to replace you.

The hardest part is often changing priorities for your future's sake. Charles told me that I needed to attend an event to see the bigger picture—that my future and all the possibilities would become much clearer. I was supposed to be working overtime that day, but he said, "Don't let 25k a year stop you from making 25k a month." He always challenged my every excuse. That's one of my driving forces to date, and a principle I thrive on and utilize with my people: being challenged.

Charles convicted me by saying "You're going to one day forget the work and money you put in, but in this industry, the work will never forget you! But it's your choice Chad."

I made the decision to call off work and show up to the event. I had a bunch of questions written down, and I wanted see who I needed to become to earn this residual money. I woke up early Saturday morning and started reading a book my mom gave me that she thought would help me with my business. As I was reading, a friend called me and said he wanted to join the next day. I was like "YES...finally! What made you decide to sign up?" I asked.

He said, "I make great money but I have no time with my family. It's not about the money, it's about the time and freedom." He said he promised his 6-year-old son that he wouldn't miss any more soccer games because of work. Even though he was happy with his check every week, he was dissatisfied with his family life. He realized he was spending more time with his coworkers than he was with his family. I didn't even remember pitching him about the benefits of time and freedom. I was only talking about getting rich. I learned right there that I must discover what others needed versus what they wanted or what I thought they needed. This was the perfect motivation I needed right before the meeting.

I rushed to the meeting, and when I got there, over 400 people were present, suited and booted. For the first time in my life, I felt out of place. I knew then that I needed a suit. I was so impressed with how everyone was dressed it made me want to elevate to another level. I looked around to learn how people shook hands and started off a conversation. Back in the day when my mom was making more money, I would occasionally attend a function with her, but nothing like this. I was from an environment in which a new pair of Air Jordans meant you were dressed up. I'd never been in an environment with millionaires and professionals of this magnitude. These were the people I was aspiring to be like, if not better. The speaker inspired me and had me fired up to conquer the world. Every time he lifted his arm, his belt showed, and it was Gucci; I wanted that. His watch was Rolex; I wanted that, too. People loved him and clapped for him and I *definitely* wanted that! He spoke about how he retired his mom and was wealthy. I know you get the picture by now but I wanted all of that, and at that moment, I married network marketing. The only way to fall in love with your future is to stop having an affair with your past.

I always look back at my success process today and just break down. I never owned a suit or a bank account worth more than $40. My first three business suits were purchased second hand off the rack at the Goodwill. I realized early that most rich people donate their expensive suits, so I went to the Goodwill on Sundays and bought some of the highest quality suits and shirts for less than ten bucks. Studies show that people's behavior drastically improves when they simply feel good about their appearance. So I felt great, looked great, and was ready to start living great. The hand-me-down suits already had me feeling like a different person when I put them on. I also wore something that was meaningful to just me. Whenever I asked myself "What if?" again, I always resorted back to my notes and stared at my WWJD bracelet that I wore every single day. This bracelet was my everything for a long time. I couldn't take it off; it went everywhere with me, even in the shower.

Once I was dressed for success, the meetings became my gas stations. They taught me that the MLM industry is just a vehicle. No matter how good or bad you are as a driver, you will always run out of gas and need to be refueled, and that's exactly what the meetings did for me. I was charged up and ready to drive. Going to the meetings and seeing people making the decision to get started by the hundreds rejuvenated my excitement. I also discovered that the only time I could practice my networking skills was at the meetings. I never went to an event without meeting someone new and exchanging information. You need a list, or what I like to call a

"Dolla-Dex," of go-getters—people who support you. I was figuring out networking, but now I needed to learn how to market since those are the two skills on which the entire industry is built upon.

The next day I called my friend who was interested in joining. He picked up the phone and said "I'll call you right back."

One day later I called again and got no answer. The next day I called, no answer. The motivation I had was stolen from me yet again. I had gotten my hopes up because I just knew I had my first partner.

I went back to the basics faster than ever after my experience with rejection. It was then that I started to feel myself improving. I discovered that just by showing up and experiencing the energy in that training room, I had tougher skin. I told myself that I was going to make it and they would know my name. At this time, no one even noticed me at the meetings and I wasn't really received well, but I knew that if I kept showing up, I would stay encouraged long enough to find my own lane. Plus, my mentor had already told me, "Never get excited about people. Get excited about production. People will lie to you. People will lose their dreams. People get distracted by life events. People make excuses. The four mental enemies are apathy, rejection, deception, and attrition. These challenges shouldn't phase you if you're plugged in and focused." You must keep saying to yourself, "WHAT'S FOR ME IS

FOR ME!" You must start recognizing, accepting, respecting, absorbing, learning, and perfecting the transition that is happening to you.

5. Keep The Faith And Good Communication With Whomever You Pray To

Understanding your mental enemies is a part of staying in this industry long-term. One secret most people don't know about me is that not only do I pray often, I also have plans to become pastor in my thirties. To consider the leadership lessons of Jesus and not include the importance of prayer would be unthinkable. Prayer and teaching are major parts of my life. To not appreciate prayer is to have an incomplete and distorted picture of how we're supposed to live and lead.

I use prayer in several ways. I am a man of prayer. I pray both in private and in public. It's my secret weapon. I use prayer to place order in my day. Even at church we learn that Jesus got up very early in the morning "while it was still dark" (Mark 1:35), to pray. It was a part of the discipline of His life. Leaders in today's hectic world can and should use prayer as one way to structure and focus their days.

There's power in prayer. When the mind, body, and soul are grateful, the universe conspires to bring you even more to be grateful for. It's also impossible to be angry and grateful at the same time. Everyday when I wake up, or right before I shut my eyes, I make my "Gratitude List." I sit down in silence and think about everything I am grateful for in my life and write it out on paper. I keep my future close to my heart, and my present moments in my mind, but I never let it stop me from hitting the reset button. Prayer and starting with the basics are the keys to regrouping. My ultimate break-through came when my friends turned their backs on me. It forced me to never seek acceptance and made me realize why I had to go for all my blessings. It wasn't about the fame; it was about the figures.

CHAPTER 6

Success:
The Creation of Momentum

I t's okay to want the light, but you can't be afraid of the dark. When nobody else celebrates your accomplishments, you must learn to celebrate yourself. When no one else compliments you, compliment yourself. It's not up to other people to keep you encouraged—it is on you. Sometimes in order to create momentum, you have to burn a bridge to separate yourself from the leeches. This kind of growth is hard because you have to be honest with yourself.

I went to work believing in myself and my dreams. I was floating, telling everyone I'd met a millionaire with a Gucci belt, and that he was willing to train me but at work, no one cared. They still were talking smack saying, "I wanna see your millions." I couldn't understand why they wanted me to make money first. All I needed was to see if it was possible. If one can do it, many can—but they were programmed differently from me, and knowing that made me stop dreaming and start hustling. Until you can separate yourself from ignorance, neglect, negativity, disrespect, and disregard, you're not ready for the next level.

Success is not for the weak. I would host meetings and no one would show. Instead of going home, I still put the work in. I presented to the empty room, in front of all the pillows, because I knew that when I did have a team, I'd be ready. People forget that the key is to 'learn and earn', but you must create moments to learn and be around your business family. Meetings manifest miracles.

In month two, I decided I had to go online with this business, and online people started hitting me up once my excitement changed. Even my friends started to see how serious I was and that I didn't need to depend on them. As I look back, one of the reasons people fail in life is that they always look for the approval of others. I was moving forward without them. Use your smile to change the world, don't let the world change your smile.

My third month started off with a new business partner. I got even more excited. My team was working, and momentum was picking up. I started thinking about doing 3-way calls. I finally had a partner who could start contributing to meetings as one of the network's top leaders. Using a third party is a sign of strength, not weakness. Weak people feel the need to prove they can do it alone, but strong people are willing to use the system and rely on partnerships to get twice the amount of work done. I started researching how to create momentum. I needed and wanted more of it. After all, I had goals and all I could see was me getting a house and a Gucci belt soon.

How you establish momentum is a reflection of your belief and enthusiasm. Next, you advance momentum. You must start working on the basics, cast your vision on where you're going, and welcome everyone you talk to and suggest they look into what you're doing. You see, casting your vision is so important. Most humans don't plan their days, so telling people that their future is or can be bright, is powerful. Leaving people with thoughts of a brighter future is called casting the vision.

Finally, you must maintain momentum. You do that by duplicating your efforts with a battlefield mentality. When I had mastered momentum, I realized that since this is a legit business I needed to start studying traditional businesses as well; that's when I discovered the *cycle of business*. Everything has a process of surge, peak, and plateau. To connect this with my new business, I asked Shatorri how she planned on getting to Diamond, which is the highest rank within the company. She said without hesitation, "I'm going to first respect my process and go after it everyday." According to Shatorri, Diamond, or top earners, go through a cycle of their own before they reach the top: terrible, below average, average, above average, good, great, and iconic.

Once she told me the cycle of a Diamond, I though, *I just got my first sign up and my excitement changed from terrible to below average.* I knew I was just getting started, but I was motivated and I figured, *right now I can't do great things, but I can do small things great!* I realized my skill level was below average at the moment, but I would be iconic one day.

It takes 10,000 hours to become a professional in any industry, and I was three months into a 3-to-5-year game plan to wealth. Since I had established momentum, it was time to advance. I started my YouTube Channel with my own vision: helping people fire their bosses. At that moment, the *NoMore925 Mentality* campaign began.

Since I knew no one who joined my team had his or her own personal vision, I had to create one for everyone to follow. Charles and I didn't have the same vision. He was all about the company, which was cool, but it was boring and I wanted something a little more fun. I had to take the sales aspect out of it because most people are turned off by a sales pitch. I wanted people to feel like they were a part of something more personal, tangible, and relatable—a movement! He kept telling me to follow the system, and I did, but with my *own* flavor.

I got to work to spread the excitement. I had t-shirts made and people were excited, coming to the meetings, and joining. They loved my vision of helping 100 families make six figures. My up-line loved it, too! Business was growing, and I hit the first rank within my first 100 days of being in business.

When I shared my story, people got even more excited about how fast you can advance. To me, it didn't seem fast, but I learned a key lesson: the more I shared other people's stories and personal testimonies, the more people would sign up. When I was starting out and hit them with the script, I didn't get anyone to sign up. It was my story, and the story of others, that got people to sign up. Stories sell, and facts tell. I felt like my job was to get the information out, so I quickly started to assist others who wanted to educate people. In the bible, it says, "...to whom much is given, much is required..." and I was ready to put in work.

Success is not always the ability to achieve, but the ability to serve through sharing. I had ranked up two times in one month! I was so excited! Next, I did my first Facebook video at my job. I told people online I was not going to be at my job forever—I had just made some money and helped an 18-year-old make more money than his dad. That video went so viral that I started getting into trouble at work because I was responding to so many emails and texts. The stories I was selling kept getting better and better. I always sold my vision, facts, and how people were already making money.

Within the first six months, I paid my girl back, created a financial plan for myself, and my bosses started noticing me walking, talking, and acting differently. I had a real estate agent, Mr. Wayne Carter, looking for a house for me. He and his wife, Ms. Portia, were super-successful and lived in a huge house. She owned a business and he sold houses—a real power couple. I wanted that life. He found me a great deal on a six-bedroom and three-bathroom house. Within six months, I was making $1,000 a week from home on top of my job income, so I bought it. It felt so great that at 21 years old, I had my first house, but I still had a hooptie for a ride because I learned a valuable lesson at 16 years old; I had invested a lot of money in a car just to have it stolen in 10 minutes. From then on, instead of spending money, I invested it. My friends from the hood were so happy for me that I'd finally gotten off that futon, that they said they would paint and help me move in. You see, when you're from the hood and move up in the world, and aspire to take others out of the hood with you, you're considered a blessing in the community.

CHAPTER 7

Success Is Not Permanent

I was totally convinced MLM would change my life. I found a way to use social media more than anything else to get my purpose out to the masses. I always post both the good and the bad news so people can see that I'm a regular guy. I also like to keep all the skeptical people who told me 'No' or said I would never make it updated on my progress. Using these tactics on social media is all it takes to create a following for online marketing. Network Marketing, however, not only generates followers, but it builds skills and relationships. Yes, there is a clear difference between the two and I knew it would be valuable to master them both. My first challenge was to find the key factors that would benefit my goals.

There are four basic rules to online marketing: be 100% authentic, perception is reality so look like money, always follow-up your likes by liking in return, and finally, embrace the masses – speak boldly and sound educated.

When you're headed to the top, not many people want you to be successful—no matter how much they smile in your face; but when you come from nothing, you have a tendency to appreciate everything. I love positive and successful people who build each other up, motivate, inspire, and push each other to their fullest potentials. Unsuccessful people just hate, blame, and complain. The trick is, if you keep putting out good vibes, good vibes will come back to you in unexpected ways.

People are jealous for so many reasons—it's human nature—but you have to protect your dreams. Sorting for those genuine relationships is key, but it's tough. Some people purposely come into your network knowing they're not for you. They have secret agendas that have nothing to do with why they joined you and your movement. Another lesson from the hood taught me that not everyone in the front row is a fan. Your biggest hater will pay the most money for a ticket to whatever you've got going on. Everyone you meet in life is for either a blessing or a lesson, so be careful! Thanks to my 'hoodar' (hood radar), game recognizes game in all aspects.

The most important way to keep making positive and strategic steps is to connect with your faith. Listen here, reader, having a great attitude goes hand-in-hand with having faith. You need both because you are going to be the biggest obstacle. Understand that you weren't born with a spirit of fear. You have the spirit of faith already, but it's hard to feel it if your attitude is unplugged from your dream, your mentor, and your goals.

Success is not permanent because even with a great attitude you can get off track, and you can only correct what you're willing to confront. You must want it more than you fear it. Most new entrepreneurs never take responsibility for themselves or recognize the moment or their habits. You have to build your knowledge base, even when you become the smartest in your circle, then take responsibility for leveraging your way into new environments. Never be the smartest in your circle. It feels good in the moment, but it's really killing your growth. Success is not owned, it's leased, and you have to make priorities and pay 'rent' often within that same month.

Don't go through life with your eyes closed or your head down. Not everyone is clapping for you. Some entrepreneurs are willing to form fake friendships and use you—waiting for the right moment to snake you and take your cookies. The transition from the hood prepared me for this type of battle with people. Corporate America also has snakes trying to hold you down and take your spot. What makes MLM better is the time and pay.

Success is a fight! You have to keep your guard up, eyes open, and ears listening to people who cross your path. Don't let people who do not have any dreams talk you out of yours, and don't let someone who is never motivated take your motivation. Don't let someone who only has one stream of income tell you how to get wealthy—they aren't part of this new chapter in your life.

Effort doesn't mean you're effective; it will most likely take you a couple of attempts to break ties with people who unconsciously take your energy. You must dig deep inside yourself and polish your skills intentionally. This is something I do consistently. Now, I wake up and look at my brand new house, and I'm happy. I've accomplished one of my goals. I'm vacationing two weeks out of the month. My passport has been stamped by six different countries in ten months, my car is paid off, I owe less than $100k on a house that I bought less than 5 years ago (I gave it to my mom), and I just treated myself and my mom to anti-gravity massage chairs worth $3k each. I can't express how great it feels to clear all your big debts and treat yourself to whatever you desire. My team is consistently growing and leads are coming in.

Because of my choice to join MLM and the contributions that I've made within my circle, I see a lot of people less stressed, spending more time with their families, enjoying life, and helping others experience the same. For this alone, I am forever grateful, but I have to reiterate that success is not permanent. With growth comes separation, and tough business decisions that have to be made, such as leaving the source where you started your business. If your departure is done correctly—with honesty and integrity—you can maintain a healthy, long-lasting relationship with your mentor and become a mentor to someone else.

Every *major breakthrough* will always come before or after a *major breakdown*. My girlfriend and I were arguing about everything, and even though I was making money, she still didn't want anything to do with MLM. I was constantly around women, having people over, and on the phone during date night. Honestly, I was just flat out busy. She wanted the old Chad back, but in all honesty, he was dead and wasn't coming back. All I focused on was my future. She wanted to move in with me, but I just needed to be alone for a while to see who I was, block out the noise and negativity of the outside world, and not bring it into my palace. I had changed. I lived by the principles of the wealthy. She was furious and I was devastated. Yes she was my best friend, but staying in unhealthy relationships is another key to failure so we ended our relationship.

Most people can't make the decision to leave someone they love while they have the energy and faith level to achieve their goals, and unconscientiously, that is why they never get to their final destinations. I knew this sacrifice would allow me to focus on my next rank, which was Diamond.

About two months after making the hardest decision of my life, my team started to fall apart. People were quitting, but I'd just upgraded my lifestyle. I had more bills, which meant more pressure. I had to rebuild my business. Now, common sense says that you can't rebuild with a cloudy mindset or you will attract other cloudy minds. So I went back to the gas station. The weekly meetings always saved my life and restored my faith.

Once, a speaker said something that I knew would stick with me my whole life. He said you have two choices in life: you can accept life, or accept responsibility for changing it.

I realized I wasn't doing the things that had gotten me my success anymore. I'd gotten comfortable only being online and not attending the events consistently. I had stopped having meetings with only one or three people there. It hit me like a ton of bricks. Signs were coming from everywhere. I felt as though a door had closed and I couldn't enjoy the fruits of my labor. This brought me back to the word leverage. If you don't have reinforcements in your business, it can feel like a job. When you do have leverage in your business, it feels like freedom at its highest level. I made it a point to be tuned into what was going on around me and see all the signs for what they were. I'd get in the car and hear a local pastor on the Rap Station saying, "Stop trying to make temporary people in your life permanent." People who get you from point A to point B might not be the same ones to get you from C and beyond. Don't keep beating on a dead horse.

At another event, I met a woman who called herself The Millionaire Maker. She said that if she made $20,000 in a month, it was considered a bad month. That was my 'Aha' moment that caused me to move to the front of the room. When Q&A started, I asked the first five questions. She had to see me because I was the closest to the stage. Every time I used to go clubbing, that was the V.I.P. section, so it just made sense that now that I was trying to be rich, I needed to be in the best seat in the house.

What do you do when your team loses their motivation?

First, she said, this happens to all of us and it wasn't just me. Her answer was a question for me: Were they a part of your core team or just your team?

"I didn't even know I had two teams."

She said, "80% is your team, and 20% is your core team. Find the 20% and work with them. Everyone will need your time, but work closest with those who deserve your time. MLM is all about numbers, not people, and attrition is going to happen no matter how good you are."

"How do you know who your 20% is?"

She said, "You'll know. Let's say for example you have a team of 10 people. The law says 20% is your core, so you find the two people who are grinding, excited, calling you, and showing up. Success is a cycle. Never think you're doing something wrong; just learn the game you're playing, and play it to win. Never get emotional. It's all about the numbers."

"How do you deal with the 80%?"

She said it's not about bringing people in, it's about keeping them in, "Just be a leader. Still serve the many because that's how you gain influence and friends, but understand you're different, and 97% of the world will never make six figures. They work for the 3%. Remember your self-portrait. The way you look at yourself determines how you act. Your similarities will create your comfort. Most of the 80% only hang around people with the same bank accounts. So all you can do is keep them inspired."

Your difference decides your importance. Be around people who make you uncomfortable until you're comfortable. If you don't know that you're different or why you are on this planet, you will never discover what others need from you. You become a hostage to what others want you to be instead of who you really are. So all you have to do is speak life into the 80%, remind them why they got started, and cast a vision that they have what it takes. Give them small assignments and give them deadlines to complete them.

When rebuilding and helping my team, what should I know?

When God wants to bless you, He brings the right people into your life. If He has you on hold, it's for a reason, or just for a season. This was the hardest pill for me to swallow. Learning to let go and understanding that it is a blessing when certain people exit your business is difficult. You make room for new leaders to emerge and allow them to perfect their skills and abilities, hence bettering their business.

Go where you are celebrated instead of tolerated. Save your energy. Protect it by being around the 20% who are more inspired, and when rebuilding, be conscious that it can take only one person to change your whole business. Only look for the few, and the few will find the many. Focus on meeting two new people a day, and before you pitch them anything, discover at least two problems they have so that you can offer a solution, which is your business. Solutions can be money, time, freedom, or control over their schedule, but you can't offer a solution unless you discover a prospect's problem. You accomplish this by simply asking a series of questions.

This was a wake-up call to my prospecting techniques and how I revised and perfected them. Inspired by The Millionaire Maker's guidance, my next step in the right direction had to do with rediscovering humility. Mike Murdock defines humility with the Law of Recognition. "Humility is not a personality trait. Humility is not intimidation. Humility is recognition of what you do not have. Humility causes you to search," which was something I didn't have and it was costing me. So from that day on, I tapped into my humility by asking questions until I understood.

CHAPTER 8

The Decision to Become a Professional

After that event, I can honestly say I was not only fired up, but I believed even bigger. I went straight to the Bentley dealership so I could experience my future. The leather was so soft and flawless. I had to have it. I went to work the next day and, like always, there were jokes: "What's up millionaire, let me hold something." I laughed, *in due time* was my reply to all the negativity.

I knew my time there would be over sooner than later. I'd made the shift in my mind and I no longer fit in with that crowd. I was a boss, no longer an employee, so I put a deadline on my last day. When I started studying leadership in the entire industry, not just my company, I started noticing trends and made a checklist of all the things I needed. A website was first on my list. Then it was a question of how I could serve the masses on my site. How could I show all my accomplishments without bragging and coming off a bit conceited?

Then I came up with the biggest idea ever! I would brand myself as a professional and offer training for free! I included it on my website because I noticed how in my Q&A sessions at the events, most people didn't have a clue. They were asking basic questions even though they had been in the business longer than me, so my thought was *they need me to help them jump-start their business.*

Personally, coaching has helped me out tremendously. Thinking with the mindset of serving the many, I was prepared to do whatever I had to do to help people win. Having an athletic background, I looked at life as a sport. I took it very seriously, and I was very competitive. To me, winning isn't *everything*, it's the *only* thing. Ask yourself how long you'd be at your job if you didn't win or perform? Winning takes talent. Winning takes character. The secrets to winning are drive and persistence—the extra energy required to make another effort. Another approach or view on life, if you don't think winning is everything, is the *hate to lose* mentality. However you see it, just go harder in whatever you're doing after reading this book. Always remember, a winning attitude matters if you want to be a professional in anything. As far as I was concerned, I needed a website fast to increase my clientele. I needed to re-brand myself as someone who wanted to help people win, because that is my passion.

At that time, I knew no one who did web design or who could help me with my brand, but it's funny how *The Law of Place* works. Murdock writes, "when you receive divine instruction, you are often sent to a specific place." I was at this random park for a cookout, and this girl came up to me out of nowhere and said, "You're Chad Thompson right? You just bought that house, Congrats!" She told me we were Facebook friends. She was inspired by me and by the way I grinded, then gave me her card. She was a webmaster and a brand specialist. Her name was Bree—a very intelligent, business-minded woman who had her own business called *BluKolla Designs*. Her grasp of my vision, along with her skills, were exactly what I needed to go to the next level. Your assignment in life is always the problem God has assigned for you to solve for others. What I had, she needed, and what she had, I needed. She gave me instructions on what I had to do on my end and it was on.

In return, she just wanted me to help her make $5k a month from home and teach her all I know about MLM. I asked her a very serious question, because I hate wasting my time, especially since it's nonrefundable. Almost every achievement began with someone finally getting ticked off and saying, "enough is enough!" So I asked her, why must you win? She answered and said, "If I don't win, I won't survive. I need to survive for my family; I need to survive for my children; I need to survive for myself." The speed of her reply and the look in her eyes came from a woman who had her goals written down. I knew this woman was serious and it's always a plus if you're as hungry as I am.

Two people can start a movement. I recognized things were falling into place, and I was so thankful to God. Next I had to find someone to take a professional photo of me, and that was simple. I posted a status on Facebook, "Who has a real camera?" and the messages started flooding in. Three weeks later, my site was complete. Boy oh boy was it professional! Not only that, it made me feel like a boss. All my friends loved it, and I told my team to start selling my renewed story.

I was just finally ready to "fire my boss", when the craziest thing happened: they laid me off! The company was going through rough times. I think God knew I would've held onto that job, so He moved me on and closed the door in my face. I was no longer working on a job, I was working on a dream.

Remembering *The Law of Place* helped me accept this new set of circumstances I was unexpectedly facing. Really, if you expect the world to be fair, you're fooling yourself. That's like expecting the lion not to eat you because you didn't eat him. You either hustle or get hustled. The *Law of Place* states that God made places before He made man, and your provision is at a place money can't buy. Money is waiting for you at the place of obedience. I am not a pastor yet, but even in the bible God instructed Abraham to, "Leave your kinfolks." You see, God always arranges your future far away from your comfort zone. I just have to believe it's my time and my turn. When they're discouraged, I always hear my team and other people's teammates say people have no money, no brains, and everyone thinks MLM is a scam in their area. I always tell them, "You will succeed somewhere, but you will not succeed everywhere you go."

The biggest secret and gut check is that the opportunity is in the man and not the land. How ironic is it that when I got a new website, a new mindset, and a brand online, I got fired from my job? I now had time to go hard with my business and put it all on the line. Life is very short, and if you don't learn what you need to learn while you're here, you can mess up generations and stop the creativity and growth in your family tree. Instead of buying your kids material stuff that won't last or get passed down, feed them knowledge, because that is what creates different realities.

Whether you're a parent or a boss, mentorship is key. Without guidance you will waste valuable years repeating mistakes and not retaining information. You can't just stand the test of time, you must also grow every year as a person. Once you master what your mentors know, you must move on and try to out-work them. Moving into my own skin and brand was exciting, but being my own boss was the overall goal. You have to use MLM to build your skills and money so you can invest in other projects outside of MLM. Being a true professional takes a good balance of being bold and humble. No matter how big your house is, how new your car is, how many commas are in your bank account, in the end, our graves will all be the same depth.

Even professionals have setbacks, but that doesn't mean you can't be successful. The way you see success from the back of your eye lids should be just as important when you wake up and go get it. It's okay to dream, but we must wake up to chase them. When you're working toward your dream, never let your part-time failures over work your full-time success. It's also very important to know that when people don't know what's going on in your life, they will speculate. People will always judge when they think they know. They will fabricate theories and spread their interpretations, and others may believe these stories to be true based on their relationship with you. What's really sad is when your dreams, intentions, and mission comes to fruition but you're hated by your peers for your growth and success or shunned if you fail.

Now, since you're ready to be a professional, try perfecting your imperfections. Every successful professional has a ritual and a set of habits. Like Lauryn Hill sings, "How you gon' win, when you ain't right within?" Success is already inside of you. You just have to claim it. This step is extremely hard because you have to address any and all issues you normally put on the back burner. It's essential to get your mind right, because what we think we know keeps us from learning.

Time is what we want most but what we use worst, so stay busy at all cost. You can't be bored and not where you want to be in life unless that's your goal. Complaining about what happened yesterday won't make you a professional, but it will turn you into a procrastinator. If you commit to whatever vehicle you choose to drive to freedom, you should never let anyone or anything deter you from it. It's your fault if the car isn't moving. You have to keep pressing the gas until it moves. The result of pressing the gas daily instead of weekly is freedom. I'm not a perfect professional. I have made mistakes here and there. I'm not always right, but I'm always real, and that's why I sleep well.

I personally believe that the devil wants you to worry about your future so you can't live and enjoy your life in the present. I ask you, is it worth the stress, frustration, angst, and self-doubt that we place upon ourselves? I say no; the devil is a liar! You should enjoy every minute of your life and live it to the fullest because it's your special gift from The Almighty. I'm so blessed to be able to open gifts daily and start each day with an affirmation that gives me life.

Being a professional takes a lot of patience. It's not just the waiting, but how you *act* while you're waiting. I know first hand what's taken for granted will eventually be taken away. That's one of the main reasons why, as a professional, you want to talk about your blessings more than your problems. No matter how you feel, get up, dress up, show up, and never give up. While they party...learn, while they spend...save, and while they sleep...live like they dream.

CHAPTER 9

Full-Time Entrepreneurship – It's a Lifestyle

The idea of life is making what happens on the inside of your mind manifest on the outside. As a man of faith, I've always believed if God could bless another man or woman with freedom, then he couldn't leave me out of the loop. After all, today is proof of what's possible if you never quit and you keep it real with yourself and your efforts. You will eventually tie up all your loose ends if you can tell yourself you deserve the results of your work ethic today.

This time of my life was filled with so many lessons and blessings. The key is seeing people for who they REALLY are. The thing that holds most networkers back from going full-time is the emotional drain of believing what others are talking about instead of believing in their own work. You are who you listen to, and you become the people you hang around. Some people are negative because negativity is the only thing that makes them feel powerful. When you don't understand that 80% of your team are only talkers, you have to be able to navigate through the social environment so that you can focus more energy on learning and building new skills.

Never study what is missing in your life; study what you possess. Having identified my 20% of hard workers made life a whole lot less stressful. Since I focused most of my time with the 20%, I realized that I had more time with my friends. They came over a lot more often for my personal balance and were always trying to distract me. I loved to party, don't get me wrong, but one day I asked myself *why am I celebrating every weekend?* I was getting into VIP sections everywhere, and in multiple states. One time I found myself in Miami one random weekend spending crazy amounts of money. I made up my mind then and there that I was not playing games anymore until I hit Diamond. See, your friendships are all investments—they create losses or gains. My hood friends were no exception; they always talked about drama and crap that didn't truly matter. Don't look at relationships with friends as potential partners, just look into them as 'your peeps' —some show you honor, and some show you loyalty. I had to sort my circle because my *hood* friends couldn't go to the level God wanted me to go to.

My life changed once I had positive influences around me and started avoiding the false path that everybody thought was normal. As you plant your flag and commit to yourself, nothing can stop you, and as you gain more skills and start understanding the rules of MLM, your mind becomes more active and more restless if you're not using it. I wasn't getting anything from the clubs anymore. It wasn't fueling my mind or bringing in new associations that would birth ideas or partnerships, which is needed when you're trying to stay *out of the box*.

Being full time was scary at first, but just being myself made this industry simple. My story inspired many new people to try their hands at being business owners, many of whom were old friends. Malik a.k.a *"El Plaga"* and I had been cool since we were nine years old, but we had gone our separate ways when we went to different high schools. When I called him to invite him to a meeting, the first thing he asked me was, "Do I need to wear a hoodie or a button up?" I told him to let go of the past and that we were about to pursue a new strategy! I had to remind him that I was on a positive path now. He came to the meeting with open arms and an open mind. Once he met The Millionaire Maker, he locked in. It felt so great to be back close with my brother and to start an empire with him.

Next was one of my football buddies. It was only until I bought my house that he was ready to talk. The conversation was so real. I told him that if he trusted me, he would sell his pistol and get the money to join, because he would never need it again. That's exactly what he did, and the local grind really got started. The Millionaire Maker never lied. She said one person can change everything in your business, and boy did it. I had pastors, lawyers, business professionals, and even street bosses hitting me up.

Even my most skeptical person on my friends list contacted me—ready to join my movement. He said, "I know I told you that what you do is a scam, but I need something different and I see you're living your dreams. Can you teach me?" Step one was to create a game plan for him. He had a super strong *why* and for the first time, he asked all the right questions. I could tell he was a leader and had been doing his research. He was on time, knew exactly what he wanted to make, and what rank he wanted to achieve—he just needed my formula. As a matter of fact, he was of a high rank in the army and was well connected. I also noticed another thing—I attracted him, I didn't recruit him. You can't recruit leaders; you can only attract them. He was so coachable and understood the power of investing money into his business. Once he came in, we made $100,000 together before we even shook hands. This was another example of the power in MLM. I want this to stick out to you: the fact that he made it all from a cell phone and a laptop in his spare time.

We had a new story to start selling, and the team went into hyper growth. People all over the country were getting promoted. People online started believing because right in their faces they had seen me, my football buddy, and El Plaga's lives change. I was so close to Diamond I could smell it. I was literally three customers away! I remember staring at the computer waiting for my title and my life to change forever. All I had to do was enter those last three names in and I'd rank up to Diamond and get a free BMW—that was one of the company perks. Finally, the moment came when I hit 'enter' and my new life began. I joined the top 3% money earners in my company. I always thank God for allowing me to learn the value in learning, making money, and expanding my horizons.

CHAPTER

10

Meet Me at The Top

The universe is never wrong. When you feel uncomfortable, you're about to have a breakthrough. When I was younger, one of our neighbors, a very successful businessman and financial advisor, invited the youth in our area to a lecture at the neighborhood gym. He wanted to teach us about money. We were confident that he knew something about the subject since he owned a restaurant, several homes, and an event facility. He had a corvette, a Bentley, and a Range Rover. He said he was a self-made millionaire and invested his money in properties everywhere. I told myself I *will* achieve everything he has, and more. After hearing his story of having no running bath water and going months with the same pants and shirts on, I realized that no matter what industry you are in, the people at the top that are performing at the highest levels all had a powerful story before the glory.

After changing the way I looked at the world and truly changing my mindset to believe everyone holds his or her own future in their own hands, I made it to the promise land. I got promoted to the top of my first network marketing company. When I hit that stage for the first time, it felt like the BET awards; there were lights everywhere and thousands of people chanting my name. You will not be let down if you keep grinding. You will forget all the work, but the work you put in will never forget you. People never chanted my name at my job.

The recognition alone was worth it, and it took me back to when I first got started. I didn't have anything on the outside, but I had everything on the inside. Flash backs of your struggle come along with your big moment. The picture of my 10" TV always flashes in my mind because that's where I started off, and now I was looking into a sea of people. I truly believe we all have the same destination, but we just have different arrival times. The things that make most people quit are the reasons why I won and made it. Save your pain and crying for the stage.

Never quit something you can't go a day without thinking about. Once you start realizing who you really are, that's when life begins, and that's what this industry does for you. It didn't matter how many leaders quit my organization. We kept pushing with the mindset of *what's meant for me is for me.* I didn't remember at that moment how many times I'd heard "No," I just remembered all the affirmatives who stuck it out and stayed until they got paid. So in eighteen months, after less than two years of nonstop hard work, grinding and getting in the mud, I accomplished things that no one can take away from me.

I couldn't believe that with faith and meeting two new people a day, at the age of 23, with no college degrees, and having barely graduated high school, sleeping on a futon with $29 in my pocket, a "good" job, hood friends, no suits, a sick mom, and all the other challenges, I had made it. I will forever appreciate all the pain, stress, sleepless nights, betrayal, heart breaks, months without making any money, and years spent with people who never truly liked me for my friendship. In July of 2012, I was not only a Diamond in the company, I had the biggest month in MLM I'd ever had! I got a BMW 750Li, and I earned $56,000. I was feeling so great—I remember it like it was yesterday.

I walked into my mom's job and told her, "Come on mom, you're no longer working a job, your son is going to take care of you!"

The feeling of victory was unexplainable because I went against all odds. Even my mom didn't believe it. At first no one but me and my business family believed. Thousands of people across the world started to believe the video of the 23-year-old kid from the hood getting a BMW and helping so many people along the way. It went viral. Leads started coming in left and right. I won't lie to you—that moment changed everything not only for me, but about me. I became more humble and cried out loud whenever I had a moment to be alone. I thought back to all the days of lack. I even revisited the many moments of almost losing my mom, and I became so grateful to God. He did all of this, and because I walked by faith, not by sight, I was able to get the promise He had over my life. I went a couple of months without making any money and still believed—that's faith. I see so many people who are waiting on a check to start believing. In this MLM world, you must believe first, then the checks will come.

When I stopped crying, the two people I called were El Plaga and my football buddy. All I said was, "Yo, they 'bout to deliver the car! Come over to the crib." Once the car showed up, they showed up.

On the day my car showed up, my old job called and said they picked up more work, and if I wanted to come back to work I could. I couldn't even believe this was all happening. I told the lady in the office, "Thanks, but no thanks." If I ever decided to work a job again it wouldn't be for money. I took a moment to thank God for my blessings, hopped in my brand new 750Li, and peeled out. It had curtains instead of tint, and extra room in the backseat with foot rests for reclining.

Now, coming from a hooptie, I had to learn the push-to-start thing, but it was so dope once I got the hang of all the features. What was even better was I had five other people on track to hit Diamond like I did.

Our team ran the company for two years straight coming in at #1 and #2 for production. I had helped break a record, and I helped a couple make it to the Top Rank in six months. We had literally cracked the code to success from home. I flew all the way to Hawaii to award the couple their Beamer. They chose the 650 coupe. Seven months after that, my good friend who had sold his pistol hit the Top Rank and was awarded a 650 coupe, too. We were forming another movement that was unstoppable—The Beamer Boys—and all under 30 years old. It's here I started to pay attention to *my* true blessing. I was getting so many calls and emails about people wanting me and only me to mentor them. I got thousands of emails from people in different companies and people who did Online Marketing. Since I had begun mastering both Network Marketing and Online Marketing, and had successfully developed a system that worked, I wanted to share my blessings, so I created my own MLM school. I put together information from my experiences and studies, then trained whoever was interested in the MLM industry.

My success and age led me to meetings that I couldn't even tell everyone about. I had chances to sit down with company owners, top distributors, and famous rappers to name a few. I was even flown out to sit down personally with the #1 income earner in MLM at his home. At the age of 23, I was looking at a man who made a million dollars every month, sitting and eating across from me, and he started when he was my age. I saw my future.

That day changed my life forever. I went from being the richest at the table to the brokest. I learned to always embrace your personal value. You must maximize your abilities and solve as many problems as you can daily in order to stay successful. As he mentored me, I discovered that my career had just started. He told me, "You will be tested now that you know the truth, and it's up to you to live a balanced life. Lead your people to that same destination." Who you are is the greatest asset. Never sell yourself short, and forget about what makes you unsure.

From age 21 to 26, I made exactly $1 million in total commissions. My first MLM experience paid me close to $800k, and my school paid me close to $160K. I was most proud of the school because I built that up and I didn't have to split profits with any company or representatives. I also partnered with a couple other projects in the relationship marketing industry that paid me as well for helping them with marketing.

MLM is just a vehicle to get you closer to your dreams, because if your job can fund your dreams, you're not dreaming big enough. It also helped me take my school from online to offline. I opened a facility called The Business District in the Atlanta area for all entrepreneurs to meet their clients, host events, or have access to their own virtual offices. I'm grateful for the key relationships I have made in the industry. Solid relationships mean way more to me than money. I then partnered up with another entrepreneur, Chris Childs. Together we vowed to help the masses starting with The Business District and created a new movement called Young Residual Millionaires Association (Y.R.M.A.). I was able to give my mom a house and I purchased her and the mother of my child brand new cars. I began to travel all over the world.

I always believe leaders don't become great until they figure out that people don't need leaders; leaders need people. Whatever your business is, nothing replaces the *Art of Fulfillment,* which according to Tony Robbins, is the joy in whatever life brings. I've been able to build teams all over the country, packing out rooms in Barbados and Mexico to name a few, and I've helped thousands of people around the world make money. I learned a valuable lesson from my mother, and that was to stop believing in everybody but me. She helped me a lot. Aside from being my very first mentor, she helps me make great business decisions. Once she turned into a believer and became coachable, we began running several successful companies together.

People always ask, "Chad how in the world did you turn $29 into over $800K?" My answer will never change, "I was always *winning in my mind*, regardless of what I was *losing in reality*." When you can revert to the feeling of faith over fear, you can make better strides in life. Trusting the process is half the battle. You have to move toward pain and action steps for your own personal growth.

The Must-Knows and Must-Dos for Success

We are living in very interesting times, especially those of us involved in entrepreneurship, brand building, and constructing winning organizations. In today's new economy, with a click of a button, tens of thousands of people can see your pictures, listen to your YouTube videos, and read your statuses. Perception is reality. I say this often because of how the public portrays us. So as long as we put positive content out there, show hope, and hold ourselves to high standards of morals, we are doing our jobs.

I use to be a wild, flashy marketer back when I first started in MLM in 2010. People to this day who meet me in public think I'm a flashy guy or sometimes even cocky, but once people meet me in person, they see that I'm humble and laid back. The bottom line is that we should all strive to live a life from which we don't need a vacation. Helping people should be the goal in today's economy, not jealousy, negativity, and hate. Listen and ask yourself, what do people say about you when you're not there? What kind of integrity do people think you have?

In order to live the life that you deserve, you must be aware enough to make the conscious decisions to get better in every aspect of your life. I know I'm not perfect. I know I've pissed some people off. I know I've got my fair share of people who want to see me fail, but guess what? I'm still happy and pray for them all. I'm lucky enough to not let all the challenges of life distract me. With every interaction, every conversation, and every experience, make sure you speak life into people. You will see your own life start change, not just by how much money you start making, but also by how many positive people are attracted into your life.

Like most things, money can be used for good or evil. The church you are attending right now was built through substantial monetary contributions. Every week, people in my old area are being helped through the kind hearts and financial ability of others. You have no idea when you're young how much money is spent on your behalf—oftentimes by people you will never meet. The day will come when you must make a decision: will you be the one who helps others, or the one who looks to others for help? It's really that simple, and it's your choice. How strong your focus is through life's countless distractions and your bounce back ability defines your legacy. You can be part of the problem or part of the solution.

If you want to be the solution, then listen carefully, because what I have to share with you now will change your entire life and generations to come. I have put in place a list of "Must Dos". If you follow this set of beliefs, you'll see situations start to change. I've broken down everything I did for the last year or so as I have been putting this book together to inspire and guide you with a game plan.

1. You must know people are important even if they don't have capitol.

If you treat everyone like one of your top clients, or you empower them with compliments and encouragement, your actions can help you live a balanced life, or what I like to call *a free life*.

2. You must know when people fall out of your business quickly and look for the people who fell in.

Stop being so emotional about quitters. Run with the runners and understand the seasons.

3. You must know that if you can't do big things great, do small things great!

Every task is important, no matter the size. Treat everything with significance and concern.

4. You must always be aware of the needs of people around you.

Make it your business to know what they want out of life. Trust me, people want to feel and know they are appreciated way more than they want to be impressed. Once you master this, recruiting will become simple because it will force you to listen more instead of hearing only to respond or pitch your business. Remember, recruiting for me didn't start becoming fun until I discovered my own swag, my own charisma, my own mojo—you can't recruit without it. Without these basic elements, you will only be able to connect, you won't be able to recruit.

Another reason why I love the industry is because anyone can learn how, and there's so much room at the top to create the life they deserve. You just have to talk to everyone everywhere, keep taking daily actions, and create a belief that every ten rejections will get you closer to your dreams. Work on your mental shift daily because you're an entrepreneur now!

5. You must always believe that failure is good.

Employees are the ones who can't afford to fail...mentally or physically.

6. You must always think your ideas out and plan for the potholes and setbacks.

Gut check moments will happen. How you respond or rebound on your worst days is what you should plan for. If you don't, you could be blindsided and panic thinking nothing will ever happen. Never stop grinding regardless of how many flat tires you must repair to define your own success. Your journey makes your story exciting once you get to the top. Remember that no matter how hard it gets, the same reason you want to quit is the same reason somebody decided to win. The following is a 2-5-year program I developed to help you plan:

Year 1
Review all of your good times, all of your rewards, trips, and failures.

Year 2
Learn and grew from all of your investments – even the ones that you didn't finish.

Year 3
Start creating balance in your spiritual life and your family life. Hang out a little more and show more of your fun side.

Year 4
Start diversifying outside of your industry – in investments and in relationships – in order to

broaden your perception, understanding, and knowledge of the industry.

<u>Year 5 and beyond</u>
Consistently review your goals and focus on the hardest ones first.

7. You must never get caught up in your own hype.
Be aware of politics and protocol. Learn how to massage relationships and always protect your environment. Your team will help you build up your reputation, so put their bank accounts first because compensation dictates behavior. People join MLM for the money but stay for the feeling. Focus your marketing around inspiration and desperation, because those are the only two reasons people join. Things only get better in life or your business when you get better. Things and people around me didn't change...I did. The downside is that people who don't grow will fall out of love with you. In the end it's all worth it, because when you look across the table, you want people around you who all brought something to the table, not just those who helped you set it up.

I know a lot more than the average 27-year-old. I've been mentored by some of the best in the industry. I've invested thousands of dollars in seminars with the best keynote speakers in the game. I've even been the Top 3% Income Earner in four different programs offline and online. I've been featured in the *Success From Home Magazine* twice. One thing that I believe holds true is that MLM is just a vehicle, and you only have to be 18 to drive legally. Do me a huge favor, whatever vehicle you choose, don't quit before you at least push it to its top speed. I mean just flat out floor it—push the pedal to the metal.

8. You must always know what to look for in the field that you're in.

You're looking for people with a great passion for life. That's very important when you're creating the culture in your business! Start off your business with managers, not cashiers. Think on a corporate level at the beginning. You're building a company, and that's why you must believe big faster. You must treat your business like you would a relationship—protect it, love it, invest everything into it, and stay committed. Never argue with ignorant people—they will drag you down to their level and beat you with experience.

9. You must never let outside sources determine your attitude.

It's not about people—it's about you. The only thing you own is your mind, and you must become what you desire. Don't base your growth on the numbers coming in or other people's promotions. This one rule alone will keep you sane in a competition sport like MLM. It's not about the harvest gained everyday but the seeds you plant everyday. You must also learn to take the blame. Most people want to be the heavy weight champion of the world but don't want to take a punch.

10. You must always lead by example.

Be the person you read about and want your leaders to follow. I had served and trained over 5,000 people at one time knowing I had never done that before, but because I was leading the way, I had to go first. I had to create my own experience ASAP. God sealed the deal when He called my name and gave me the vision that MLM, not my job, would make my fortune. Your response is different depending on who calls your name. You must learn how to respect people and allow your up-line's voice to speak to the language of your soul.

What Does Hard Work Look Like?

Y ou didn't wake up today to be mediocre. Hard work is a term that's used so much it often goes in one ear and out the other. Also, the term 'if it ain't broke, don't fix it' holds a lot of people back. Your life is constantly under construction, and there's always room for improvement. Being from the hood, they always said if you come into this world, it's not your fault, but if you live the rest of your life broke, it is your fault. Nelson Mandela said in one of his speeches, "There's no passion to be found playing small—in settling for a life that is less than the one you're capable of living." Amazing things happen to your life, and your rise to the top will be easier if you let go of negativity.

But you can't rise to the top without breaking a sweat. So what does hard work look like? That's hard to explain in a few sentences, but one example is when rich people live like they're broke versus broke people who stay broke by living like they're rich. I once debated for a whole plane ride with a woman about the subject. She told me that it was all about the choice to keep changing, and I agree with her because it took me back to when I heard one of my favorite rappers of all time say, "Everybody looks at you strange, say you changed, like we worked this hard to stay the same." Hard work is commitment to a task and staying focused. Just do whatever it takes to become a powerful and inspiring example.

Sometimes in life, situations keep repeating themselves until you learn your lesson. It's hard work to remain positive and stay uplifted. I remember going to Orlando to open a market, and this older woman who was meeting me for the first time asked me how I stay so positive. Why did I smile so much? She told me that I really couldn't be that happy.

I told her that coming from where I came from, I talked a lot of smack to people and started a lot of fights back in my day, but I made a promise to God that if he would deliver me from those bad situations, I would get my act together and do the right things for the rest of my life. You don't have to be negative for attention. Being overly positive sticks out more. No one has ever made himself great by showing how small someone else is.

She laughed and said, "So you really like your life, huh?"

I paused and recollected the Biggie Smalls verse, "Damn right, I like the life I live because I went from negative to positive." As I walked away from the lady, I realized she probably didn't believe me anyway from the look on her face, but I just kept smiling. I only grow apart from people who don't grow and have no desire to do so. That doesn't mean that I treat people differently; it's just something I kept from living in the hood. Once I lose respect for you, it's gone. I never re-respect someone who has refused or neglected to change.

Some people don't like me because I won't give them respect they haven't earned, love they don't deserve, and trust they can't keep, but I'm okay with that. I'm a businessman who still remembers everything he learned from the streets and all of his mentors. I also know I can't do epic things with basic people, and I'm cool with that. Hard work for you should be finding ways to incorporate this book's nuggets into your daily lives. Try for the next thirty days to think, talk, act, walk, smell, and feel like you have the *NoMore925 Mentality*, and watch your business and life explode. On your rise to the top, you will cry, lose friends, feel pain, and even think you're going crazy. Just keep going and trust that everything will change. The rebuild, believe it or not, is better than the original grind. The end will justify the means!

You really know you're a hard worker when everyone around you makes you 'The Example.' I find that because of my age and experience, a lot of parents want me to speak to their children. Being an example adds big value to your life and the world as a whole.

Now that you're almost done with this book, I hope you can better determine where you want your life to go. On your rise to the top, be careful who you emulate, pretend to be, or copy; you might forget who you really are in the interim. You already have what it takes to rise to the top right now as you're reading this. DNA has nothing to do with success. Turn your genes into overalls and get to work. Staying busy is what hard work looks like, and only those who (like me) are willing to risk it all, or even go too far, can possibly find out how far one person can go.

Become more than your name badge and title. Use this book to help the generations coming up after you so they can rise to the top. My generation really thinks hard work is about staying fly on Instagram and spamming people's newsfeeds on Facebook. In our current times, social media is running the world so we are naturally hooked. That's why we must reduce our TV and internet time and substitute it with more reading time. You have to be ready to grind 12 hour days with no results.

The Twelve Steps of Hard Work are simple:
1.   Network
2.   Get up early
3.   Stay focused
4.   Watch less TV
5.   Read more books
6.   Avoid time wasters
7.   Invest in your health
8.   Take calculated risks
9.   Write down your goals
10.   Work smarter – not harder
11.   Do something you believe in
12.   Foster meaningful relationships

Key Techniques to Build a Team of Hundreds

Team up and do living room events with people outside of your group. Keep your people skills up. You can check the talent and eventually become the talent outside of what your up-line's coaching. It very important to your career.

You must find these three types of people: entrepreneurs, knowledgeable people, and pioneers. *Entrepreneurs* are hungry, and they need to feel the energy from people, but not all entrepreneurs are leaders or are good with people. That's why understanding partnerships are important because you have to form an inner circle and learn how to leverage relationships. You don't have to have it all or know it all to win...just network and leverage.

Knowledgeable people have the ability to think, which has nothing to do with leading, but when you can get things done in-house, it makes your overall team grow faster and creates value for your personal team brand. A *pioneer* is willing to do anything first. Being first isn't the same as leading; you just need a person to strike action with the group besides yourself. You should treat this person with respect always, too, regardless if they ever hit a rank or not. Pioneers are trend setters who lead from the front. Five thousand people joining in 40 days verses 500 people in 40 days is a big difference in leadership. That's why in all of my coaching classes I tell people, "I help smart people make great decisions."

I believe that people don't join us for what we do. They do it for why we do it. MLM didn't touch my mind at first, it touched my heart, so I got started, so don't disguise humble beginnings. There are a lot of broke professionals and rich amateurs. So with that being said, do exactly what you should do, and do it with excellence. Worrying doesn't take away tomorrow's troubles, it takes away today's peace. I do think MLM is for everybody. It takes hard work, but so does your job. It's a valuable stream to have not just because of the money, but for all the business, financial, and mental growth as a person you will endure. It is a life-changing experience. It's not a get rich quick scheme, but let's be real, who wants to get rich slow?

The Structure of MLM Companies and Understanding Money

I love the industry with all my heart. It changed my life forever. But you must never forget that you *don't own it*, it's only your database, so it's important you understand the 4 Phases MLM companies go through:

Phase 1: Ground Floor
Start-Up Company

Phase 2: Formulation
Gathering The Success Stories

Phase 3: Momentum
Name is Buzzing in the Public

Phase 4: Stability
Company Has Built a Solid Platform

Making your first $100k or even $800k starts with your understanding of money and your emotional disconnect with it. You must learn to let go of greed and the fear of losing money if you want to achieve wealth. You must also understand how money works in general—the four fundamentals about money itself include: the power of supply and demand, how the credit market works, its importance on the economy, and the concept that residual income is mandatory.

It is very important to understand all these things because without this simple understanding, everything you read and hear online seems like a scam or miracle. Most people who hear of other people making money think you need a large amount of money or a huge following to start, or often say they simply can't afford to risk anything. They're comfortable remaining in their fairy tales of winning the lottery, marrying rich, becoming the next big rapper, or baller. These hopes, wishes, and dreams are easier because their mindset is to take the elevator rather than the stairs.

There is a victory in the valley, and I'll prove to you that needing money and a huge following is the wrong mentality. That's why I needed to get my story out there for the world to know that it is possible to turn $29 into $800k. Thinking you need this and that to be successful is nonsense. This excuse is no different than choosing not to start a traditional business out of fear that no customers will come and the business won't make it. It's the same as simply refusing to buy a house because property values might drop, or you can't stand the thought of having to pay a maintenance man if something goes wrong. All of these are excuses people use because they have no tolerance to take a risk and they have the wrong mindset. MLM is for the needy and the greedy. Successful people recognize opportunity faster than unsuccessful people do. Stop talking to those who you think need money and talk to those who want it! You will be amazed at how fast your business will grow.

Hard work is part of being an adult. When I was a kid, I couldn't wait to be an adult, but when that time came, I lost most of my freedom to things like jobs, bills, being politically correct, fitting in with the latest fashion, and even trying to impress the boss by talking differently. When I was a kid, all I had to do was go to school, get good grades, do my chores, and stay out of trouble. That's what I called an awesome life. I wanted to make a lot of money so that I could be a kid again and rid myself of freedom stealers and enjoy freedom again with childlike faith. That's why hard work is important. I'm very passionate about no one giving me anything. I want to earn everything I have. That's what hard work sounds, looks, smells, feels, and tastes like; it embodies and encompasses your entire being!

Payton Manning said in an interview, "The NFL never gave me anything, I put the work in. I studied game tapes while other athletes were out spending their wealth." He said he does a lot of community work to be around kids full of passion because it motivates him. Personally, I can teach a person with passion one skill and they can win big, and I can teach a person with no passion all my skills and they remain a chump. You can't turn a poodle into a pit-bull.

Freedom over everything is my motto! People all over the country always ask me, "Chad, how are you always the #1 recruiter in all your programs?" It's because no matter what city, state, or country I'm in, we all want one thing and that is freedom. Freedom is a universal language. So if you talk that talk and your work ethic backs up your voice, you'll never run out of people to share your opportunity with. Hard work and knowing when to save your energy is key to long-term success.

There is a declining market for words. The only thing the world believes is behavior. Act with wisdom and grind your butt off. God gives every bird its food, but He does not throw it into the nest. Think about it reader; He makes everyone and everything work. In the jungle it's eat or be eaten. In the real world, it's boss or get bossed around. It takes intelligence to conceive an ideal, courage to try it, and persistence to make it work. Nothing in life is free—not even air. I created my future so I can't be mistaken for a regular guy; that was my passion: to escape the rat race and teach my family the *NoMore925 Mentality*. Life is all about growing wiser and limiting your losses. Some people fish with a pole—I fish with a net.

This chapter was put in my heart to share because I know that even as a leader, it can be hard sometimes. So many people are looking to you for energy, not even realizing you're human, too. It's very hard to give energy and inspire people when you don't have energy or are not always inspired yourself. It's hard to give your team tools and scripts you're not sure of, familiar with, have no knowledge of. Even if you don't have a down-line of 300+ right now, this little nugget will still help add value to your calls and organizational skills. This book has almost all of my proven success tips and I assure you that most of them have never been shared before.

When it comes to your energy, you must protect it with your life. One important way to protect your energy is to understand with whom you're working with and who's really building your down-line. Remember, this section of the book is for professionals who want to rise to the top, so if you're not there yet, this tip is a leg up.

My coach taught me in 2011 that in business there are *wanters*, *needers*, and *deservers*. When leading a small or large organization, you will encounter these three types of people 100% of the time regardless of what little you give them.

Wanters always say how much they want. They want success, they want to be where you are, they want to be on stage, they want, want, want, want! However, their actions don't reflect their words, and their feet don't ever move. You still help these people, you still support them, you still do all you can to help them win, but until they prove to you that they are major players, you focus on other leaders. Major players are part of your 20%.

Needers tell you all their problems, issues, drama, and talk about how much they need this to work, they need this to pay their bills, they need this to pay for their home. They desperately yank for your help. Like the *wanter* above, their actions do not reflect their words. They tell you how hard they are working so you dedicate extra time to help these people. You support these people and care about these people; however, you're building a winning team. A winning team needs major players who are running like crazy to build their business and to build their dreams.

Now truth be told, I was very needy being a mama's boy. That was something I had to snap out of. I also remember a lesson I learned when I was 17 years old and driving my mom's car one night. (Not taking away anything from my mom, but she has had some hoopties in her day and that's why I made it a point to bless her when I made it big with something she never had...a brand spanking new car). I remember picking up this girl in one of my mom's hoopties, jumping on the expressway, and then the car broke down! My car had broken down many times before and I would just stick my finger out, catch a ride, and dealt with the situation, but here I was with a girl, broke down, and embarrassed. My first reaction was to start cursing, but then I noticed the girl looked frightened and she kept telling me to calm down. She said her dad's shop was at the next exit where we could get a tow truck, and it would be all good. I had to tell her to hold on with the phone call to her dad because I didn't have money for a tow, to fix the car, and to take her out to eat. This made me even more mad and I started pushing the car and yelling even more. Then I noticed something more powerful than the predicament. While I stood there waiting for assistance, I noticed that no one stopped to help, but when I started pushing the car, two cars pulled over to help. The moral of the story is, sometimes when people see that you're helping yourself, they're willing to help you, too.

Deservers are future leaders. These guys and girls get things done. They focus on money-making time, and you rarely hear their excuses. These people go above and beyond to show you how bad they want it, not by their mouths but by their actions. The *deservers* earn the majority of your time, energy, and efforts. These are the people who build teams into thousands. They are the ones in your group you can fully trust, depend on, and hold accountable. The deservers drive your groups and business to new heights and new levels. These people eventually become your family. They understand and are really satisfied and content with the challenges of the process. They always begin with the end in mind, and they go the extra mile and do whatever it takes to get the job done. I love working with *deservers*. Always remember you're building a championship team; you work with everyone, but you build with who's building.

Your number one freedom tool is your phone. Here's a secret for you to write down on paper and tattoo onto your brain: even leaders have trouble dialing for dollars. The phone can feel like a thousand pounds, or the smallest distractions can magically become huge distractions. You then tend to put everything in front of working that freedom tool. But really, every dream or goal you've ever had is waiting in front of your faith and behind your fear. You aren't allowed to conceive something you can't achieve. So one of the tools I tell new MLMs to get is the 'easy button.' You can get one from any office supply store. The purpose is to make hanging up that phone a whole lot more fun. It also decreases the fear you feel between when you hang up and when you make another call. I call that *operation repeat*. You have to bang out five straight calls back to back. You can't have confident conversations until you discipline your disappointments. My first mentor never treated me like a broke bum, even when I really was. I don't treat others like that either; because of my background, I respect everyone regardless of their station in life. I DONT SEE POVERTY, I SEE POTENTIAL in people.

It's very important that we ask ourselves what can we do today to start the process, and a huge part of that is picking up that phone. I had to lose it all to understand it all. That's why I'm trying to save you time, stress, and energy. 'Life has no remote; you have to get up and change the channel yourself'. That saying goes for business as well as life. In order for you to double the size of your team, you must double your freedom tool usage per day.

I wrote this book because if you have a book full of must dos and don'ts, and certain mandatory laws to follow, even when the motivation wears off, you can still win with facts from this book. Motivation is what gets you started. Obsession has to take over and fuel your drive, and the only thing that can keep you focused and motivated is habits. Habits keep me going. Replace your bad ones with habits that are success-oriented or wealth-related, like pressing that easy button and getting in the habit of making calls less stressful and more fun. It almost becomes like a game because at the end of the day, it's only numbers, and you can't get emotional over numbers. Every time you close a deal, get a customer to hit the button. Every time someone tells you they are not interested, hit the easy button and remember *operation repeat*.

A good script to use over the phone is simple, and you can find one to use for any network marketing companies online or via text. I want to teach you the *law of the lid*. Your team can only grow as big as the leader. You must never max out in knowledge or stop learning new skills. In order to have a down-line of 300+, you can never stop learning. Your mentality has to shift from looking up to your mentors for everything, to never wanting your team to go anywhere for knowledge but to you. Of course you want them to have other mentors so your voice doesn't burn out, but if you stop learning in this new economy, you're left behind. On your rise to the top, God will never give you a dream that matches your budget or your knowledge level. He's not checking your bank account—He's checking your faith.

Focus on Winning – Not Structure

Every few days I get up and look through the Forbes list of the richest people in America. If I don't see my name, I get to work. "If you can see it in your mind, then you can hold it in your hand," the late great Walt Disney said. You have to see it first—this is all part of recruiting yourself.

Ask yourself, do you see the people screaming your name already? Even if you can't see their faces, you should see something. Can you feel the stairs press against your feet as you walk up to the stage? Can you hear the people calling your name as you get your awards? Here's a tip you will need: silence. In order to meditate or focus, you need peace. The goal is to visualize it. Be alone long enough to paint the picture and see the trail of your victory. People think this step can be skipped and only focus on structure and other things. This is a part of winning; this is a part of gaining the *NoMore925 Mentality* and seeing your future. This is all a part of rising to the top in your personal life.

I refuse to leave behind excuses—if your past was tough, work to make your future better. Do not repeat the same mistakes, whether they are yours or someone else's. We have to see it in our minds to believe it. Your motto this year, and every year moving forward should be, "I know what I want and I'm going to get it." Remain focused even if you're stuck on a task—just do it and keep going. Until now, that past life hasn't been what you wanted or needed. You have no reason to stop grinding, reader, you have to know what challenges look like. You have to know what pain feels like. Most of all, you have to know what small victories can do for your heart. So just stay focused, and follow through with whatever project you're on.

Sometimes when you practice being alone, your circle decreases in size but increases in value. The *NoMore925 Mentality* can be described as focusing the full power of you on what you have a burning desire to achieve—the "I can't even think about looking at my past" attitude. Reputation will penetrate into your unconscious mind and force you to believe.

You will not find many days of luck on your journey to the top. Most people never answer the phone when opportunity rings. So if you have said no to everything for years, switch it up and say yes; it's ok to challenge yourself. Go back to the person who told you to read this book and tell them you're ready to give their business a try.

You have to take your hands out of your pockets in order to climb the ladder of success and rise to the top. Once you finish this book, something that has been draining you for years is about to dry up and lose power over your life. With the *NoMore925 Mentality*, you can expect a turnaround in Jesus' name! Now say it out loud and walk in faith. You've got this! Get out of that survivor mode mentality, have faith, and watch your blessings rain down. It takes money to make money, so how much are your dreams worth? Once you learn your true value, you won't give people discounts.

Trust me, you can learn all the techniques, but if you don't believe in yourself, nothing will happen. I've been blessed to find people who are smarter than I am, and they've helped me to execute the vision. My biggest mistake when I was a newbie was not making enough mistakes.

Here are a few, quick, final thoughts. If you have a problem with making time for things outside of your job, or even working on things that are not your job, you should repeat this saying: *this is my day to be great!* Being flexible is also necessary. Try doing weird things so you can experience weird results. Honestly, making 20k, 50k, or 100k a month is weird, not normal, so you have to be like that to attract that income into your life or bank account.

Explore how you can improve the quality of your life or the service you provide. Your value to the marketplace relies on how much you have learned from other people during your rise to the top and how you amaze your customers. By being one of those people who keeps his commitments, and being relentless, you show the example of determination and focus. People love that, whether they give you credit for it or not. Think about it like this, everyone likes flowers, but most people hate weeds. Weeds don't need encouragement to grow. They grow through the cracks in the sidewalks. They are annoying. If you want to grow orchids, there's a certain process you go through. They won't just grow through the concrete without encourage-ment.

Personal greatness is going against the tide, and even though set backs will be there in your face, you must maintain the *NoMore925 Mentality*. Stand up for your dreams, peace of mind, and health. How do you rate yourself from 1-10 when it comes to being self-motivated? We grow from people and projects. How much motivation do you need to do a lot or a little? That's important to monitor because the time is ticking.

We can't help getting older, but we don't have to get old. Take care of yourself and step it up. Most families grow apart because of money problems, so I ask you, are you and your family living together, or are you dying together?

Most people are really just existing and not living or thriving. Don't go to the grave with good stuff still in you like ideas, talents, and boss moves that haven't been revealed or acted upon. You know when you're super motivated and when you're passionate to get to a goal. It wakes you before your alarm clock.

Knowing it's possible to go from $29 to $800k with only Wi-Fi and a dream shouldn't sound so far fetched now. I need you to believe that you run the jungle and you're a lion. I'm rooting for you if no one else is. Besides, a tiger doesn't lose sleep over the opinion of sheep. I encourage you to be the hope for your family, and be okay with others not embracing your transition after reading this book.

People who are intimidated by you talk bad about you in hopes that others won't find you appealing. They are only insecure with their own situations. The only thing you can do for them is pray. Even if they don't like you, I guarantee they will be checking on you and all your social media pages religiously to see how you're doing. Every man and woman has the ability to work hard, but they don't ask God to help guide their footsteps. Personally speaking, I won't ever stop grinding until they make pillows that feel better than money in my pocket. Then and only then will I sleep better, but until then, you can bet your last dollar that Chad Thompson will be working.

AFTERWORD

To everyone who is a leader, a boss, a go-getter, or a top money earner in the MLM industry: it's our obligation to mentor, coach, and pour value into the people who are coming up next in the ranks. The newbies are what some people on the inside like to call the 'little people'. Looking back on my career, I can give you names of individuals from different companies who poured into me, and some who completely blew me off. I'm thankful because when I did ask top earners questions, most of them never gave me irrelevant information. They shared their secrets and expanded my knowledge to some degree. Coming from the block, a lot of people would never help me, so my mission was such a refreshing and powerful concept; there are people who will help others and expect nothing in return.

I've also learned a lot from people who made millions of dollars in other industries. One of my mentors has crushed several companies in a two-year time frame. I even had a one-on-one, in-home sit down with the #1 earner in the entire MLM industry. I've never made either of them a dime, but they are always there for support if I need it. That's why even till this day, I put out so much free content online because it's how I came up in this industry— by building solid, trusting, relationships first.

When someone needs help, regardless of what team or company they are in, help them. Always think about the little guy. In my first MLM company, I had up-lines who questioned this technique of being friends with other reps in other companies, or even sharing techniques with them. My advice to you is to never forget that this whole industry is about relationships.

It's hard to listen when you're not humble. Most up-lines, if they brought you into the business, they don't want you to outgrow them, or out rank them, so remember you're in business for yourself. It just so happens you're not by yourself.

Nothing in this book is guaranteeing you anything. It's just letting you know it's possible. Thank you for reading. I didn't want to make it too long because I want it to be an easy read in hopes my story will inspire someone. I wanted to let folks like me know that degrees don't determine success, and if you believe in yourself, anything is possible, but it takes hard work.

This book is long over due. People around the world have been asking me for years to put my story on paper, so here it is. I wanted it to be filled with real-life inspiration and business principles that helped me shape and design my life. Now if you follow my lead and pick up some of my mentality tips, you are not guaranteed anything but a step closer to living a free life, so act as though you are a boss and believe it's coming.

I had a lot of fun writing this book. I wrote it all on my iPhone from the heart. I am very thankful to be in a position to even write a book. I've been able to acknowledge God in front of thousands of people. When I decided to write this book, I also wanted to put in place a guide for you to always come back to so you can try to figure out which principle or chapter applies to your situation.

NoMore925: Secrets to a Free Life is very valuable and has unique information that you may or may not ever need to use, but at least if you give this book to a prospect or another up-and-coming entrepreneur, they will have the know-how.

I'd also wanted to share what I felt was some valuable information that I know is seldom (if ever) focused on in most training sessions. I hope you find it as valuable as I did. For years, people have used my story to help build their business and have told me I needed to write a book. Well here it is. From all my files, recovered notes, every roadblock the devil set before me in order to delay this process, it's finally accomplished. Volume 2 of *NoMore 925* will be coming out in late 2017, so be on the look out for more nuggets on what to do once you've made it. I will explain how you can and should maintain your blessings and multiply them tenfold, but for now, it's back to the grind and helping people all over the world become more than their haters want them to be and more importantly, more than they ever imagined they could be. My Facebook Formula for 100k Online is available at www.mlmclasses.com. I would love to hear your feedback and what you loved most about this success guide.

Thank you for your support and I'll see you on Volume 2, but until then, have a great day on purpose, and I'll see you at the beach or the bank!

—Chad Thompson

Self-Awareness Questions

1)   How many people does it take to start a movement?

_____

_____

_____

2)   How many recruits does it take to explode your business?

_____

_____

_____

3)   What can you do to be a more active participant of the 20% team in your group?

_____

_____

_____

4)   What keeps people fired up and their gas tanks full?

_____

_____

_____

5)   List 3 things you're up against for your breakthrough.

_____

_____

_____

6)   Every time you go to a meeting, what are you supposed to do, and why?

_____

_____

7)   What 3 things are you grateful for?

_____

_____

8)   What are your top 3 weaknesses?

_____

_____

9)   What were 5 main things that stood out about MLM that interested and intrigued you?

_____

_____

10)   What do you do when asking for help?

_____

_____

11)   What is something you need help with now?

_____

_____

_____

12)   How can I appeal to their self-interest?

_____

_____

_____

REFERENCES

Greene, Robert, and Joost Elffers. The 48 Laws of Power. New York: Penguin, 2000. Print.

The Holy Bible, New Living Translation. Grand Rapids: Zondervan House, 1984. Print.

Murdock, Mike. 7 Laws You Must Honor to Have Uncommon Successes. N.p.: Wisdom International, 2009. Print.

Robbins, Tony. "BREAKTHROUGH." Tonyrobbins.com. Robbins Research International, Inc, 2016. Web. 1 Apr. 2016. <https://www.tonyrobbins.com/personal-development-process/>.